APPALACHIAN HERITAGE

VOL. 43, NO. 4
FALL 2015

ESTABLISHED IN 1973

PUBLISHED QUARTERLY
by Berea College
CPO 2166
205 N. Main Street
Berea, KY, 40404

www.appalachianheritage.net

 Periodicals postage paid at Berea, Kentucky, and at additional mailing offices. ISSN# 03632318.

 Thanks to bell hooks for her gracious permission to reprint "Writing Without Labels," which first appeared in *Remembered Rapture: The Writer at Work* (New York: Henry Holt & Co., 1999).

Electronic submissions only at www.appalachianheritage.net

Distributed by the University of North Carolina Press. Basic subscription price: $30/year for individuals, $40/year for institutions. For subscription requests and inquiries, visit the magazine's website, email uncpress_journals@unc.edu, or call 919.962.4201.

CONTENTS

BOOK REVIEWS

COVER PHOTOGRAPH

EDITOR'S NOTE

JASON HOWARD

In her memoir *Bone Black: Memories of Girlhood,* bell hooks writes of growing up in small town Hopkinsville, Kentucky, in the 1950s—of a girl "young, gifted, and black" who finds refuge in books, who creates a secret world, who notices the roles women and men play in her culture. It's the story of her "girlhood rebellion," of what she calls "my struggle to create self and identity distinct from and yet inclusive of the world around me."

This battle is one that has defined hooks's life and career as one of the world's leading feminist intellectuals, cultural critics, and creative writers. It has played out in the more than thirty books she has produced, in the countless lectures she has given on university campuses across the country, and in her own life. As the only black undergraduate from Kentucky at Stanford University in California—where she wrote what would become the landmark book *Ain't I a Woman? Black Women and Feminism*—hooks faced derision over her rural accent and country upbringing. She sought solace there from the natural world, looking for reminders of her beloved Kentucky hills in the landscape surrounding Palo Alto. Subsequent moves to Wisconsin, Connecticut, and Ohio reinforced her sense of self as a "country girl." The struggle continued after her move to New York City, where she wrote and taught for many years, but where she also felt a profound disconnect from the culture of individualism and "intense anonymity" that she believed devalued community. In 2004, she returned to her native Kentucky, serving as Distinguished Professor in Residence in Appalachian Studies at Berea College and finding the sense of belonging that she missed in her years away.

All these years later, hooks is still leading a rebellion, offering thoughtful—and often provocative—critiques of popular culture, giving readers moments of meditative beauty in new poems and essays, and moving academia and the wider culture towards a discourse grounded in the notion of intersectionality: how oppressive systems of misogyny, racism, classism, homophobia, transphobia, and others work together.

As this year's featured author, hooks and I have curated a mini-anthology of sorts that showcases the range of her work, including a craft essay, a poem, a conversation, and an unpublished novel excerpt. In her essay "Writing Without

Labels," she calls for a more inclusive definition of literature, one unconstrained by categories of race, class, and gender. Her poem "Wheel of Life" showcases the "universal witness" that has always marked her writing. The conversation with actress and advocate Laverne Cox covers a wide range of topics, including images and film, spirituality, the influence of family, and hooks's legacy. Finally, hooks has delved into her archives and given us an excerpt from her unpublished novel *Sister Ray Seeks Salvation*, in a passage that features the title character having an internal, stream of consciousness dialogue about gender roles, objectification, desire, sexuality, race, social mores, and the role of the artist—and facing a moral dilemma around these issues.

In addition to new work from hooks, this issue of *Appalachian Heritage* also features sterling stories from Jessi Lewis and Lydia Munnell. Essayist Beth Newberry meditates on "The Curve of the Smoke," while creative nonfiction writer and poet Leatha Kendrick contributes a revelatory essay about Appalachian poet Effie Waller Smith. Poets Divya Ramesh, Kathleen Lewis, Jane Sasser, Lucien Darjeun Meadows, and others offer moving moments of lyricism.

"Appalachia is my fate," hooks declared recently at The Appalachian Symposium—held in September at Berea College—proclaiming her sense of belonging. May you find glimpses of yours in these writings. ■

bell hooks

WRITING WITHOUT LABELS

BELL HOOKS

When I was a girl longing to be a writer, the writer whose work most touched my soul, reaching into the innermost places where much within me had gone unrecognized and unloved, was Emily Dickinson. Even though I had my card game Authors, which gave me a visual portrait of her, I never saw her as a white woman. Reading her work I never thought about race or sex. Even though I was stealing away to the privacy of our attic rooms to hold her words close in a real world of racial apartheid that affected my life daily, determining even where I could walk and eat and sit (the colored-only section at the movie theater), when it came to words on the page all this was forgotten. Intuitively, I understood that the persona of the writer was not as important as the words that grip, hold, and transform. I read other women writers. Their work did not speak to me. Clearly, I had not chosen Emily Dickinson because she had been born woman. Her vision resonated with mine. She evoked those emotions I felt but could not talk about with anyone. It was all there in her words.

The girl I was who longed to be a writer had been well schooled in the belief that art transcends categories. In our black segregated schools we never made a writer's race primary. It was always the work that mattered. Even if it was noted that we should give special attention to Langston Hughes's work because he was writing about a world we knew intimately, we also knew that shared racial identity and even common experience would not lead one to produce great writing. To become a great writer one had to be able to move deep into experience, into emotion, into life. Dickinson's field of vision made contemplation of metaphysics, of religion and nature the space where she experienced life to the fullest. While her race, gender, and class had shaped the outer boundaries of her experience, inside she lived unbounded. She lived in service to the imagination. She had surrendered. That was the mark of the great writer: the willingness to surrender to the power of the imagination.

When I began writing poetry in girlhood utterly under the influence of William Wordsworth, Gerard Manley Hopkins, and Emily Dickinson, I dwelled only on the big issues, the universal concerns of life—death, love, sorrow, joy. Writing was a place where I could leave behind the ordinary mundane pain of my life. Imagination allowed me to move through and beyond this pain. I did not want writing to be the place where I told my story, where I confessed—I wanted it to be the paradise where I could forget the daily experiences that led me to certain emotional states. It was the emotional state that was the place where the imagination would find its treasures, not concrete experience. This is the reason I did not focus too intently on race, gender, or class.

In the realm of the concrete I did confront being black, female, and working class. I confronted it in the privacy of a domestic world where my longing to read these poets from another time and faraway places was not fully understood. I confronted it all the more when I let it be known that I wanted to become a writer. No one tried to dissuade me from writing; they simply talked about what I would do to make a living. Writing, in their eyes, could be done when one came home from work. It was not that they did not respect writing. It was that they saw it as having nothing to do with real life. To everyone in our world words on paper were magical. They filled me and those around me with awe. Even then I understood that doing the real work of the imagination required time—space to dream, contemplate, and talk with spirits, space to prepare oneself for the sacred rite of putting words on paper. I was not at all interested in making a living. I thought then that my destiny could be just like Emily Dickinson's. I could stay alone in my little house and write. Of course as a young girl believing in magic I did not think in concrete terms about how I would acquire the house, the means to survive. I thought it would happen like magic. I let no one dissuade me from my dream of becoming a writer.

I held on to that dream even as the concrete world of race, class, and gender began to impinge upon that imaginary space I created for myself where all was possible. In the all-black schools of my childhood there had never been any doubt that we had equal access to the world of the imaginary. No teacher had ever looked upon my love of reading and my longing to write with scorn, ridicule, or contempt. No one had ever suggested that being black, female, or working-class would stand in my way. No wonder then that I cherish the memory of those all-black schools where no one ever thought my love of Dickinson and Wordsworth was strange, where no one ever questioned my right to love great literature no matter who had written it. Racial desegregation changed all that. In the white school smart black people were suspect. Even though my teachers nurtured my longing to write, it was there that I first learned that I would confront barriers—that there would be folks who would not be able to take writing by a black author seriously.

Even then I understood that doing the real work of the imagination required time—space to dream, contemplate, and talk with spirits...

In high school, I began my search for black writers. To this day I remember the incredible sense of ecstasy that I felt when I first found an edited volume of poetry by black writers. There in that slim little book I read sonnets by Countee Cullen and Claude McKay. I read the short beautiful poems of Georgia Douglas Johnson, a kindred spirit who I knew in my heart must have read and loved Dickinson as I read and loved her. Finding the work of these black poets affirmed that I was not a freak, a special aberration. It was so inspiring. It is truly difficult to find words that will adequately convey what it was like to suddenly be forced to study in a world of white authority figures challenging everything about the world I had known before coming into their power. That white world made me doubt myself. And in the space of that doubt I needed proof that they were all wrong—that there are great writers who happened to be black, just as my beloved Emily Dickinson happened to be white. Despite the fact that it was hard to find published writings by black authors, I found my proof and I was set free.

I often think about this time in my life when I hear contemporary debates about whether the identity of the writer matters. Rarely are those who want to insist that it is only great literature that matters willing to acknowledge that in a culture defined and organized around principles of race, gender, and class domination, identity matters simply because structures that silence and shut out are already in place to assault the consciousness of anyone who dares to live by the belief that we are always more than labels. It was not the world of segregated blackness that sought to deny me a place of transcendence where the content of my writing would be deemed more important than the color of my skin. The world of whiteness imposed rigid barriers. The logic of that world, of white supremacy, had to be resisted. To the extent that I was always struggling against racism, race mattered. Making sure that it did not become the issue that mattered most or the only issue that mattered was the burden placed on me. Assimilating into mainstream white culture would have been the easiest way to flee these difficulties. I could simply live as though I were white. Issues of race and racism could be conveniently ignored or dismissed as irrelevant. One of my favorite writers, Jean Toomer, had tried to escape the burden of racial identity by passing. Ironically, this choice blocked and deadened his creative imagination.

When I am at my desk writing, I always think of myself as a writer who is a black woman. I never think: I am a black woman writer. Race and gender are made to come first in the world outside, where if one is from a marginalized group anything about you that does not conform to white male norms is acknowledged first and foremost. Even when a black and/or woman writer is praised for not calling attention to race or gender, these categories are still being highlighted. Deviance from expectation is no escape. Writers from marginalized groups are usually faced with two options: overidentification with an identity or disidentification. In actuality our realities encompass the complexity of being both a writer in the best and most transcendent understanding of that vocation and being individuals whose work is informed by the specifics of race, class, and gender. William Faulkner is a traditionally accepted "great" writer who is one of my favorites. As a professor of American literature talking about his work I usually emphasize the larger themes of that work: death and dying, lost love, failure to achieve desired dreams. Yet there would be no way to adequately talk about his vision without also acknowledging that the perspective of the fictional South he created was definitely shaped by his race, gender, and class. Clearly, those identifying labels matter; the fact is they do not matter in some absolute way. Writers who seek to flee any reference to identifying labels of race, gender, class, or sexual practice often do so because the tendency is to make too much of them. Yet to act as though they have no importance whatsoever denies all of us the opportunity to have an expansive understanding of the influences and passions at work in the writer's imagination.

In her nonfiction British writer Jeanette Winterson goes to great pains to disassociate herself from the label "lesbian writer." Positively, she endeavors to lay claim again and again to that space of creativity where any committed artist is more concerned with the work than with identities sexual or otherwise. In "The Semiotics of Sex" she declares: "I am a writer who happens to love women. I am not a lesbian who happens to write." However, while she goes to great pains to critique gay thinkers for acting as though sexual identity is important, she does not painstakingly critique heterosexist thinkers for refusing to approach work that focuses on differences in an unbiased manner. Sound and beautiful writing is not the only reason Jeanette Winterson's work found both acclaim and a sustained audience. Were it not for the activism preceding the publication of work like hers challenging heterosexism, done by individuals who openly identify as gay and by their allies in struggle, there might not have been any mainstream audience, however large or small, capable of appreciating Winterson's work. While she is right to castigate any individual who approaches her and the work concerned only with what she or any writer is doing sexually, she oversimplifies the issue when she implies that no mention should be made of homosexuality.

At no point does Winterson suggest that writers should not be required to speak about their sexuality. Such thinking would not curry favor with mainstream critics. No one would balk at a critical reader of the work of Henry Miller or Norman Mailer, both white heterosexual male writers, who made reference to their autobiographical comments about their sexuality. Indeed, these comments illuminate the work. At times it appears that Winterson objects to any mention of sexuality if a writer is gay. Any writer should resist any attempt to see their work solely as a reflection of one aspect of who they are.

Winterson is on target when she insists that "to continue to ask someone about their homosexuality, when the reason to talk is a book, a picture, a play, is harassment by the back door." Yet at times it seems that she wishes to deny that sexual practice in any way influences work. Her comments are mere mimicry of the elitist tone of generations of white male writers and critics who though writing very specific and autobiographically based work insisted that it was always and only universal. In fact, really great writing is usually both specific and universal in its appeal. Winterson's comments often seem to be oriented toward currying favor from a mainstream traditional critical public. With heavy-handed didacticism she contends: "Art must resist autobiography if it hopes to cross boundaries of class, culture...and...sexuality. Literature is not a lecture delivered to a special interest group, it is a force that unites its audience. The sub-groups are broken down." Does Winterson seriously believe that centuries of heterosexual writers never included openly gay characters in their fictions because they were resisting autobiography? The truth is heterosexuality was infinitely more familiar to them. To the extent that they were writing from a foundation of what they knew, they were writing autobiographically. It is utterly pretentious and false for any writer to act as though only gay writers, and writers from other marginal groups, have indulged in merely describing their reality. There is infinitely more autobiographically-based bad writing published by heterosexual writers. The desire on the part of any writer from a marginalized group to emphasize the aspect of their reality that has previously been aggressively denied as a result of political repression is natural. And even though a consequence of this may be that the reading public is often offered writing from that group which is shallow, poorly crafted, or sensational, the breaking down of social barriers that once precluded the telling of such stories makes it all the more possible for great writing to emerge. When writers from marginalized groups do work that is truly marvelous, this writing is not seen by dominant audiences as personifying the group's capabilities. Usually it is seen as a rare exception. Yet if there is a marvelous book by a straight white male writer and ten trashy books by the same, this group's capability will be judged by the better work.

Ironically, the power of great writing by a writer from a marginalized group to inspire and influence the work of emerging writers from that group is diminished when such an individual disassociates their work from that of peers from similar circumstances. Concurrently, this disassociation tends to reinscribe the assumption, rooted in already existing biases, that this writing and the writer represents an exception. Individual writers from marginal groups often invest in the idea of their specialness. They may feel threatened when aspiring writers seek to do equally compelling work. Black writers often feel pitted against one another, especially for

I fantasize, as many writers do, of writing a book where no mention is made of my race or gender—where the work has to be considered on its own terms...

attention from white-dominated mass media. When planning the marketing of my most recent memoir, a white woman publicist commented that I might have difficulty gettingreviews in publications because another black woman writer was publishing a memoir at the same time. My first response was to call attention to the fact that at least six white women writers had published memoirs at the same time and magazines had no trouble focusing on all of them, sometimes in articles that addressed their work individually and at other times collectively. She agreed that this had happened but that "it just does not work that way for black writers." Again it is not the black writer seeking to ghettoize but rather the racial biases of mainstream white press that make it evident by such practices that only one of us at a time can expect to receive attention.

To counter racist agendas at both the editorial and public-relations level, I fantasize, as many writers do, of writing a book where no mention is made of my race or gender—where the work has to be considered on its own terms. To fantasize this is to imagine a publishing world that no longer exists, if it ever did. Now more than ever the persona of the writer is as much a feature of marketing strategy as is the work's content. Doris Lessing exposed this when she tried several years ago to get a book published using a pseudonym. The manuscript deemed worthless and discarded when seen as written by a nobody was eagerly snapped up when Lessing revealed she was the writer. Whether the labels attached to writers and marketed are identifiers of race, sex, or some other characteristic that sets the individual apart from others, it is always limiting to be defined by one aspect of one's identity.

The black and/or female writer who publishes work that specifically focuses on race or gender issues will often find that their writing on all other subjects will be ignored. To be labeled the "feminist" writer means one is likely to be excluded from any acknowledgement that you are someone capable of writing about topics that extend beyond this marker. Equally so, to approach feminist publishing with the desire to do work that does not "fit" with the prevailing tone and temper of the movement is to also be excluded. Even though we are living in a time when the rhetoric of the house embraces multiculturalism and diversity, writers who are not straight white males who resist confinement to any category or subject matter in their work often find themselves reinscribed into limiting confined spaces by mass media. Unfortunately, the language of mass media is not a rhetoric of complexity; the more complex the vision the harder it is to convey in a short interview, brief comment, or book review. When a writer has a body of work the critical reader may only have looked at the one book they are discussing but on the basis of this one text will assume that they fully comprehend the scope of the author's concern. The more marginal one's group status in the culture, the less likely work will be given serious attention by mainstream media. Often press who are hostile to feminism deny any woman writer with this label attached to her work quality time or attention. As a black woman professor and writer who writes about the politics of representation, I am well aware of the extent to which white women readers are seen by the mainstream media as the only meaningful audience for writing by and about women. As a consequence, if a black woman writer writes work that specifically addresses black female experience, the tacit assumption will be that the work has no appeal for white females. However, it is always assumed that books written by white females specifically about their experience have universal appeal.

As a reader I find I am wholeheartedly able to identify with work by white women even when it does not address the experiences I am most familiar with. For example: Erica Jong's witty autobiographical account of aging, *Fear of Fifty*, highlights growing up white and Jewish. Her personal stories delight me even though our backgrounds are in no way similar. The difficulty lies with mass media not realizing that white women readers are interested in work by black women. This is especially true of mass-market women's magazines. Of course only white women writers can write about their specific experiences without ever having to describe themselves as white. When I first published my memoir, *Bone Black*, I kept describing it as a memoir about girlhood that emphasizes growing up black and southern, among other experiences. Again and again editors tried to describe it solely as a memoir about black girlhood. I resisted this so as not to imply that nonblack women could not relate to the experiences I recall. The large number of letters I received from white women readers who identified with the experiences I shared was yet another reminder of how empathy allows us to understand another's differences.

If all writers consciously used identifying labels in ways that describe without defining we would be able to see the larger picture both in relation to an author's vision and her personal story. In the case of Jeanette Winterson, I read her work before hearing any information about her person, her nationality, race, class background, or sexual practice. Later I was pleased to learn that she was from a rural working-class family that had difficulty accepting her love of reading because that is an experience akin to my own. No large numbers of successful writers come from working-class rural backgrounds. The extent to which that formative experience shapes a writer's vision fascinates me. I can value this bit of information without allowing it to overdetermine my reading of her work.

In all my years of writing I have never heard any writer from a marginalized group insist that readers should only read gay writers if they are gay, black straight writers if they are black and straight. I do not know where to find writers who are so attached to labels. I hear about them most in the works of conservative thinkers who are condemning their narrow-mindedness, their failure to understand that great literature transcends race and gender. In her collection of essays *Skin: Talking About Sex, Class and Literature,* Dorothy Allison shares again and again that her work as an activist for lesbian and feminist movement never led her to assume that she would write from a limited perspective. To her and fellow lesbians whose writing she admires, "literature was about refusing all categories." Allison remembers one of her teachers, Bertha Harris, declaring: "There is no lesbian literature, she told us. The relevant word was literature, real literature that came out of an authentic lesbian culture." Concurrently, there is no black literature, only literature that conveys our experience as black people. There is no feminist writer, only the writer who writes from a feminist perspective.

I and all the writers I know want to be respected first and foremost for our work; the root meaning of the word respect is "to look at." Writing can be considered on its own terms and then it can also be looked at in relation to a writer's background and personal history. My experience as a southern working-class black female from a religious family has shaped the way I see the world. Yet the specificity of that experience does not keep me from addressing universal concerns. It is not an either/or issue and never has been. Both in our past and present the tyranny of race, gender, and social biases has meant that disenfranchised writers have had to struggle for voice and recognition in ways that highlight identity. That struggle has not ended, as we must now resist the form recognition takes when these categories are then deployed to confine and restrict our voices. If long-standing structures of hierarchy and domination were not still in place and daily reinscribed, calling attention to a writer's race, gender, class, or sexual practice would illuminate work, expand awareness and understanding. I am not a writer who happens to be black. I am a writer who is black and female. These aspects of my identity strengthen my creative gifts. They are neither burdens nor limitations. By fully embracing all the markers that situate and locate me, I know who I am. Writing the truth of what we know is the essence of all great and good literature. ■

WHEEL OF LIFE

1.
The wheel of life turns round and round
all hope alive in still presence
a steady heart of compassion
sacred ritual giving peace.

2.
One drop of water flowing into the ocean
wet with enlightenment
a taste of eternal presence
of morning dew, of night fall
reincarnated dream.

3.
Pure aspirations dark tara
jewel of the most high
open the heart's door
bear universal witness.

4.
True nature of self-abiding
darkness and light, male and female
a sacred mandala past and present
a tantric path that calls and liberates
all eternal Buddha.

5.
Thread of tantra
bind mind and heart
imperfect being choosing to perfect love
radiance of Buddha light shining.

BELL HOOKS

bell hooks and Laverne Cox

photo by Ebony C. Motley

BELL HOOKS: A CONVERSATION WITH

LAVERNE COX

Earlier this spring, bell hooks invited the award-winning actress, producer, and advocate Laverne Cox to speak at the private opening of The bell hooks Institute, a new center in Berea dedicated to critical thinking and contemplating the intersectional issues of race, gender, and class. The choice of Cox as the institute's inaugural speaker was no accident. A native of Alabama, she leapt to worldwide fame in 2013 as the hairdresser convict Sophia Burset on the hit Netflix show *Orange is the New Black,* making Cox the first transgender woman of color in a leading role on a mainstream scripted television show. An Emmy nomination and the cover of *Time* followed, and Cox soon realized that her newfound success and fame also brought great responsibility. Since then, her work has expanded beyond the small screen to college campuses across the country, where she brings an empowering message of transgender equality and living authentically.

When they met in New York, both hooks and Cox sensed an instant connection. Cox had long appreciated hooks's work, which she had studied and applied to her life and craft since college. For her part, hooks had admired Cox's "humane" portrayal of Sophia on *Orange,* as well as her fierce advocacy and embrace of intersectionality. After an onstage conversation at The New School, hooks decided to bring Cox to Appalachia.

What follows is an edited version of their lively conversation at The bell hooks Institute, which covered subjects ranging from the power of language and images to fame and fearing corruption.

■ ■ ■

BELL HOOKS: When I [heard about] *Orange is the New Black,* I was like, "Ah, I see some problems with it." But there's only one character I really love, and that is Laverne Cox. And I felt that the relationship between the Sophia [Cox's character] and her wife was one of the most humane couplings—the way they dealt with conflict, the way they talked things out. And I thought, "This is something we don't normally see on television." And so to me—despite all its other things I could rap about...I felt like this was a magnificent intervention. *[looks at Cox and grins]* Hey, Laverne Cox.

LAVERNE COX: Hey, bell hooks. So I don't know bell well. We just met for the first time last fall...but we all are here because we have a relationship with the work—this work that has truly transformed so many of our lives. It certainly has transformed mine. There's so many moments in your work where you talk about being transformed, about being made over in more liberatory ways. I think it's in *All About Love* that you write "the heart of justice is truth-telling." And telling the truth has been a hallmark of what you've done for over thirty years...I've been doing a college lecture tour for over two years now. It's called *Ain't I a Woman*. And of course I talk about your work every time I stand up before college students, and talk about how you talked about intersectionality so many years ago, and how it's really crucial to understand how these systems [of racism, sexism, classism, homophobia, and transphobia] work with each other, and how we can begin to move beyond those systems.

I discovered your work when I was a college student, through my brother...*Black Looks* was the first book I read, and then this was the second one, *Yearning: Race, Gender, and Cultural Politics*...And this particular paragraph, this repeated phrase stayed with me for so many years. bell writes:

Often when the radical voice speaks about domination we are speaking to those who dominate. Their presence changes the nature and direction of our words. Language is also a place of struggle. I was just a girl, coming slowly into womanhood, when I read Adrienne Rich's words: 'This is the oppressor's language, yet I need it to speak to you.' This language that enabled me to attend graduate school, to write a dissertation, to speak at job interviews carries the scent of oppression. Language is also a place of struggle...Dare I speak to oppressed and oppressor in the same voice. Dare I speak to you in a language that moved beyond the boundaries of domination? A language that will not bind you, fence you in, or hold you. Language is also a place of struggle. The oppressed struggle in language to recover ourselves, to reconcile, to reunite, to renew. Our words are not without meaning. They are action. A resistance. Language is also a place of struggle.

That's one of my favorite moments from you.

BH: That bell hooks is just a damn good writer. *[audience laughs]*

LC: When I was re-reading [your work] this weekend, I remembered my own college days, sort of struggling with identity and who I am, and trying to come to voice and critical consciousness. And I thought about how your struggle is so evident in these words, and how in so many ways you still feel like that young girl to me, sort of struggling to come to voice. How do you feel today, as there's a bell hooks Institute around language being a place of struggle?

BH: When my sister Teresa died, at a very young age—I have a hard time talking about it—but one thing that struck me was that I needed to take care of my legacy. She did not take care of her legacy. She did not take care of her body. She did not take care of herself in ways that would have carried her into the future. She died a horrible and painful death when she could have died in the comfort of her home with one of the most wonderful institutions in our society—hospice. And it really brought home to me that I needed to take care of myself. And my legacy. My work. And what really struck me is, as I began to tell people that, they were like "bell, you don't know what you're doing." You know, "you need to give your papers to some white institution." You know, "some black institution like Spellman."

And one of the things I said is, "I don't want black people to have to go somewhere where they have to go through surveillance, where they have to show ID, where they have to go through a metal detector to get to the work of bell hooks," because my work has always been about liberating us and liberating our stories...

In those early days, before I had as many books as I do now...I wrote, I read. But as I grew, as the writing grew, as I grew to have the blessing of my books being taught—in every institution practically in the United States—I was no longer this, you know, kind of hidden treasure, I had to come to terms with the world. I have been obsessed—because of my colleagues wanting me to give a sermon on resurrection—with Simon, and that passage in Luke where it says: "Simon, Simon, Satan has asked to sift you as wheat. But I will pray that your faith will not fail; that you will turn around and strengthen your brethren."

So for me, it has been a constant struggle to keep the faith. So when I hear that Laverne Cox, with all her blonde tresses and the like...[is] informed by the work of bell hooks, it's important because this is the ordinary person—and let me tell you, she was ordinary before she became gorgeous new black star—

LC: —I still am.

BH: She told [me]...that for a while she couldn't pay her rent. That's over with.

LC: Praise Jesus.

BH: Even though she works in the belly of the imperialist-white-supremacist-capitalist-patriarchy, she continues to work with the work. And that's what I'm passionate about. How does the work go into the lives of ordinary people? How does it go into the places where we would never think about it going, and have an impact on people's thinking and their lives? So tell us a little bit about that, girlfriend.

LC: Amen. For me, as an actress, obviously part of my job is advocating for trans folks, and often trans folks of color. And so much of the work of yours that really impacted me was the way you read film and media culture. And it shaped me... many years before I started taking acting seriously. I was a dance major in college, of all things. And when I started my acting training...[teacher Susan Basdon] has this thing where she's like, "What do you want to say to the world about this character that you play?" And so, doing that very intensive study, I brought in bell hooks's work, in terms of the ways in which I read scripts. It's not only about bringing in a walking talking human being, but how do we create subversive moments in the work as an actress?

There's limits to being an actress, I gotta tell ya. There's a lot that I can't do there, but what I'm really also proud about is my work as a producer. I got to produce a documentary for MTV last year called *Laverne Cox Presents: The T Word*, that looks at the lives of seven trans youth between the ages of twelve to twenty-four-years old. And we got to tell their stories. And so being at the helm of telling these stories of marginalized people, I was like "How do we break with traditional ways of telling these stories"? And it's MTV, and there's limitations... Working with these institutions that don't always value black life; working with these institutions where you have to fight to have more than one black person on a television show. And to tell these stories in ways that don't objectify, that fully humanize—this started with my reading of your work. And it's an intense fight...

And that piece—"we cannot go into the journey as objects and try to emerge as subjects"—that quote from [Brazilian educator Paolo] Freire that you quote so often—how do we not objectify trans bodies has been so crucial to the ways in which I've tried to go out into the world as a trans woman...People [who] objectify us want to reduce us to our bodies or surgeries that we have or have not had. And how do I walk into spaces as a full, whole person? That... has come from your work.

BH: Well, I mean one of the things—as I've watched all these episodes of *Orange is the New Black*—I thought the show was really evil. The only redemptive character in the whole show is Sophia because of how she deals in a just and kind manner... So what I like to think of how the work is going to totally change Laverne, so that one day she will produce more and more work herself...I think that we really need you to produce more. What do you think about that?

LC: We're working on a new documentary now that I'm executive producing...called *FREE CeCe!*...about a young African-American trans woman named CeCe McDonald who spent nineteen months of a forty-one month prison sentence in a men's prison for defending herself against a racist and transphobic attack that happened on June 5, 2011.

And the night of the incident, CeCe was walking down the street—they were going to the supermarket. They were having a barbeque the next day. They passed a group of white folks outside Schooner's Bar in Minneapolis. And this group of white folks outside the bar were drunk. And the first thing that CeCe heard, in terms of the racist transphobic and homophobic assault, was the "N-word"...and then a fight ensued. One of her attackers ended up dead and, of course, when the police arrive—CeCe is bleeding out of her cheek—they arrested her on the spot and charged her with murder... She's out of prison now, I'm happy to report ... and the documentary is about her story [and] the culture of violence against trans women. And her life has been challenging since she's been out. She's had some lovely moments of being honored, and traveling the country speaking, but she still has a felony conviction. She's still struggling...

BH: I mean, one aspect of Laverne's trans activism that is very much a model is that she herself embodies intersectionality. Because just as people would ask me why I would want to talk to a Laverne Cox, they might say *why would a Laverne Cox want to talk to me?* I mean, there's not many of those Hollywood movie stars knocking at my door saying, "Let's have a conversation." So it is her willingness to stand for justice, not just for trans folks, but for anyone who is in need of justice.

LC: Well, what your work so clearly illustrates is that the injustice for many of us happens at the intersection of multiple identities. When CeCe was attacked that night, she was not just attacked because she was a trans woman, she was also attacked because she was black—and because she was a woman. So all of these things are happening at the same time. And if we just look through a single identity lens, we're not going to really get the full picture. And that is, I think, one of the wonderful gifts of your work and part of your legacy—that we can really look at the interconnected nature of imperialist-white-supremacist-capitalist-patriarchy. I add to that: CIS-normative-heteronormative-imperialist-white-supremacist-capitalist-patriarchy. These forces are constantly working in tandem with each other and, you know, because of what I do, I understand that I'm working within this system. There's limitations that I have at this point in my career... But this piece of knowing that there are people who've come before me who stood for justice is very inspiring. I think we all stand on bell hooks's shoulders.

BH: Well, tell us a little bit—how has fame changed the life of Laverne Cox, besides being able to pay the rent?

LC: Being able to pay the rent is amazing. I'm still in the same apartment. Seriously, though, before I booked *Orange is the New Black*, I had done several independent films in 2011—like seven independent films. I was like, "Yeah! My career is turning around!" Then 2012 comes and I don't book anything for like six months. I had a restaurant job, but I wasn't making very much money in the restaurant, so I was in rent arrears when I got the job for *Orange is the New Black.* I was on a payment plan to pay my landlord a certain amount of money out of a month so I wouldn't get evicted. So that's where I was just a few years ago. So I'm very grateful that the rent is paid now. I mean, honestly, I don't think I'd be here if it weren't for *Orange is the New Black...*

BH: Do you find that people get pissed at you when they feel like, "Well, what are you talking about? You're a movie star and you're making lots of money."

LC: I did *The View* the day after—or I think it was the week—that the Darren Wilson grand jury testimony of Ferguson came out. And I was like, I can't be on *The View* and not talk [about it]...I mean, in this grand jury testimony, Darren Wilson talked about this demon coming out. And it was just so—I can't even repeat it, it was so horrible what this man said about Mike Brown. And I had to say this on television, and people were tweeting all kinds of—when you talk about race in this country, what has been really deep to me as an out trans woman of color is that transgender issues—yes, a lot of people have issues with that still, and come at me with all their hatred or ignorance or whatever—but with race, it's so much deeper.

BH: Wow.

LC: And I think I lost some fans talking about Ferguson, and telling that truth the way I saw it. So it's deep. It's really deep...

BH: I mean, this is a good thing because our work, our lives, are different. You have to always be conscious of the camera, and what's going to go out in the world about you...because of the impact. And your work is teamwork in a way that bell hooks's work is not teamwork. You know, I say what I want to say. I choose my battles. It's a very different kind of work. How do you deal with that?

LC: It's tricky. I'm very careful about what I say. I've said a lot today, all things that are truthful. And I always try to speak the truth, but I'm also very careful about what I say because

I understand that it's not just about me, that I have a lot of firsts by my name at this point in my career. And it is bigger than me. So I try to be really intentional with language...I don't always get it right, obviously. And I'm a human being. And I have to allow myself to be human, and to have human moments that...may happen in the public sphere. I do it imperfectly, but I'm really careful.

BH: So do you fret about—you know, everywhere you turn, we see you. You're doing something. I've already told her I'll make my appearance on whatever news show she has. Do you fear corruption?

LC: I do...I've had moments when...there was this show I was involved with, and I was involved with several partners on the show, and this network was like, "we want to do this show with you, but we're not interested in these partners you have." They came up with the idea for this show all together. And I was like, "No, I'm not going to do that." I was able to bring them along with me. I think that was a moment when that corruption—it felt like this really intense moment that you see you see out of a movie was happening to me...It's definitely something I think about and I try to be vigilant about. It's hard. I just try to continue reading my bell hooks, and continue to stand for what it is I believe in. And I try to pick my battles very carefully. The corruption piece is real, though. What is brilliant, too, about bell hooks's work is that you remind us that each and every one of us can become an oppressor. We all have that capacity. God help me. I hope that never is me...

BH: Well, what do you think is the most positive intervention of *Orange*?

LC: I love that there was a moment in season one when we were shooting the rap-battle scene. It was in the common room, and I looked around, and there were like over forty women in one room...There were senior citizens to early twenties. There were plus-sized women. There were women of multiple races. Gender identities. There were various queer women. I was just like, I've never seen this on television before. I've never seen anything like this, with this kind of female diversity. And for me that's really exciting. And I think our audiences are really responding to that kind of diversity, as well as the way our stories are told.

BH: You can critique me, as others have. I was very, very disturbed when—what's the name? The evil one? The evil black woman?

LC: V—

BH: V is run down—

LC: I don't see her as evil, first of all.

BH: But run down. Because to me, the image of her with her hands in the air very much echoed that of Michael Brown. And the thing that pissed me off...was that she was rude. And I think that many of us as powerful individual black women are often beaten down and harassed because some white person sees us as difficult or rude. So I found that very troubling. Can you deconstruct that? Many people tell me, "bell, this is the kind of projection you do. This is why we don't like your work." *[audience laughs]*

LC: What I think, for me, one of the wonderful gifts of your work is that, I think it's in *Yearning,* where you talked about how you were critical of Spike Lee's work, but that criticism came out of love.

BH: Don't know about the love part. *[Cox laughs]*

LC: Or interest—

BH: —Generosity. *[audience laughs]*

LC: Generosity. Thank you. *[audience laughs]* I always encourage people—students come up to me all the time and they ask me about Beyoncé, or whatever, and because of your work, I always encourage them—yes, you can consume this stuff, but never do it uncritically. And so I deeply respect the fact that you are very critical viewer—that you have an oppositional gaze that deeply informs the way that you see. And I feel like that perspective is deeply necessary. As an actress on the show, I can't agree with it. *[audience laughs]* But I obviously deeply respect it. We've had this conversation before, and I'm still here.

BH: Well, I think that we don't address the power of images. I'm trying to work on a new book that's called *Spirit Talk,* and I'm talking about how when [my family and I]...went to church every Sunday at Virginia Street Baptist Church. There was a huge mural behind the pulpit: white Jesus with his hands out, the world in front of him, and the black and brown people at his feet. I'm trying to write about what do we think is the impact of that image on us as young black children that we saw every Sunday?...And I'm writing about the fact—many of you know I consider myself a Buddhist-Christian, and Buddha comes in all colors, all genders. I feel like when I came upon Buddha through the poetry of Jack Kerouac and Gary Snyder, there was something so profoundly liberating that we weren't dealing with the image of a white man, or even of a colored man, because there's so many different formations. And I don't think we do enough with, "what is the impact of an image on us?"

LC: What I would say about *Orange* in light of that is...we see the 'V' character as one character who we lose in a sort of horrific way, but we have seen so many other black women on this show, though, that we have different relationships to, as an audience that we can look to, and be inspired by, or laugh with—

BH: I agree with you—

LC: —or feel connections to.

BH: But that doesn't mean that that image where a white-skinned person is running a black woman down and saying she's rude as though, you know, "Kill those rude-ass black bitches." I mean, that's how I read it...

I've been trying to critique *Doc McStuffins. Doc McStuffins,* as some of you may know, is the first crossover black Disney kind of image, but I notice, as I was buying my *Doc McStuffins* paraphernalia—you know, the Valentine cards were eighty percent off—was that she's always carrying that white sheep or lamb or whatever. At first, you know, being a black woman, I was like, "Why is she carrying that little white baby?" And people were like, "Oh, it's not a white baby, it's a lamb." But again I thought about our visual processes. You know, how many white people still feel that as black women we need to be Mammy and we need to take care of them? Do you know of that?

LC: I know of it. I don't watch. And I don't think I'm the target demographic. *[audience laughs]*

BH: Well, I mean, so once again, as I try to talk to people about this, especially parents, they acted like, "Oh, bell, this is the problem with you—you're just too extreme." And I tried to get people to think about, when you're looking at the visual from a distance, you can't tell that it's an animal—when you're looking at it from a distance, it looks like a little white baby-doll...

I remember as a girl telling my mama, "I don't want no white doll. I want a doll that looks like me." Mom...found this doll [that] came with a little diaper and a bottle, and you could put the water in her, and she would pee out of the little hole. That was fascinating for all of us...I was a brilliant child, I named the doll "Baby."

Growing up in Kentucky—so racist, in racial apartheid—but...I can tell the world the roots of who I am came from the hills of Kentucky. From the black church. From Mom and Dad. I mean, and I'm critical of Mom and Dad—everybody can tell you that—but I'm also respectful of all the foundation that Mom and Dad gave us...

Let us hope that we will live into that justice that Martin Luther King talked about, but let us not forget about the power of images. And even myself...when Satan says to me, "Well, I don't think you need an institute, bell. You ain't all that…Who do you think you are?" I always remember, you know, when I went to college, and these white boys pulled me—I was out with some white man I was dating—they pulled me off the sidewalk, and they said, "Nigger girl, what are you doing with a white man? Who do you think you are?" And you think about those imprints, those assaults, and how—for a long time—that stayed with me. It was echoed by teachers, by different people, by the man I thought I loved…

And so I think that it's because we have to know who we are. And we have to live in the strength of who we are. That, for me, [is why] this institute is important for Kentucky. For young black girls—for all girls. To recognize—as Toni Morrison always said, she wrote *The Bluest Eye* because she never read a book that featured a young black girl. And she… wanted to put that black girl at the center.

Growing up in Kentucky, black people were not at the center. Our land, stolen. So many painful things happened to us. We are not just the Wildcats. Cause you know how the white people worship ball players until they do something that they hate, and then it's like slavery time, plantation culture all over again. So we have to be more than that. We have to have institutions where we are self-determining.

LC: And at the center.

BH: Yes. Even if it's hard. ■

SISTER RAY SEEKS SALVATION

BELL HOOKS

It was all pretense. She knew it. He knew it. She could feel he knew it by the deep unhappy look of utter withdrawal she would catch in his eye, just at the moment when he would begin a hearty laughter-filled conversation with someone. It was high school all over again. Ray went to the party because she knew he would be there. He would be there because the party was for him celebrating his birthday. It was at their house because they welcomed any excuse to have a party. Although she wanted him to notice her, she had not bothered to dress up. She wore a faded purple sweatshirt over a long sleeved pink T-shirt and another lavender colored T-shirt could be seen sticking out from the top. She wore her glasses, old blue jeans. She wanted him to notice her but she wanted not to care at the same time. Anyhow, she told herself, "wasn't she out hunting, wasn't she stalking prey, and didn't that demand disguises." She was wearing the perfect disguise. He paid her no attention. He was always surrounded by people congratulating him, drinking. She saw in him then all the things she did not like. The pretending to be happy with people you were not happy with—that he was even having this party hosted by someone who hated his guts.

She watched the women who hung about him, noticed their white flesh, one so white she reminded her of bleached bright cotton sheets hanging on the line—the kind she had to spend hours hanging on the line as a child. She had hated those sheets, the cold that burnt her fingers, the wet melted snow seeping through her cheap shoes. The memory of that whiteness was tinged with hatred. Ray brushed it aside not wanting to think about it, not wanting to allow her feelings to get involved and cloud her judgment. She was here to observe, to record the facts. She was here to be the hunter who can shoot straight. So she noticed that the really white woman, with the long dark hair, the husky voice, a foreign accent but she could not tell from where, carrying around with her a smell that reminded Ray of sheep; that made her crave for the smell of fresh-cut grass, was trying too hard, making too much of an effort to be looked at, remembered. Ray was making a note in her imaginary workbook. "Fucks women, probably prefers fucking white women, especially those that come back for more, that beg for more, even though what they had was not sufficient, was not enough." After making these notes she then looked around the room counting the women, not she decided whom he had fucked but who had fucked him. There were about six. They were all white. They were all trying too hard.

"Wait," Ray told herself. One was not trying very hard and she wasn't even sure that he had ever had sex with her. She seemed to be asking him to give her a chance—to try her. They stood in the kitchen talking with two other people, talking about women's issues, something about whether women had the right to do the same kinds of things men do. Ray liked this woman. She too was white, dark-haired and spoke with a thick foreign accent. Ray heard her name Zvia but found it difficult to say. She practiced it over and over again in her mind but she could never get it to come out right, so she gave up, assuring herself that she would never see this woman again or any of these people—except him. Still she liked her and liked watching her, captivated by this discussion that was all about feminism, women asserting political rights when Zvia's body politic was saying just the opposite. It was having a conversation about seduction. It was saying to him I desire you. I bring you all my fantasies about the black man who fucks so good, who gives it to you as you have never had it before, who makes you come and come again. He was enjoying it and brushing it aside the same. The body in question kept coming back for more even pleading as it was brushed aside. Ray found it a beautiful body. She was amused by it and the body's fascination with him. He for the most part was soaking it all up, wallowing in it the way pigs wallow in cool brown mud on a sunny day. But what Ray was trying to understand from the way he stood and the way he kept taking small sips from his glass in between the talking, was why he did not accept the gift of the body offered him, why he was so thrilled, excited, perhaps even wet in his pants but was all the time saying no.

Saying no by the way he kept his body at a distance from her, by the way he managed to avoid touching her even as she made gesture after gesture that would make parts of their bodies meet. He was saying no but Ray was sure his penis was hard, was panting like a mouth saying not only yes, yes but saying please. Well behind the sexist garbage he was putting forth on the subject of whether women should have the same rights as men, he had another mouth that was saying please only it was saying please don't tempt me. I'm not worthy of you. I am so afraid of failing you. Ray was recording it all, and all the time acting indifferent, trying to be attentive to the hunter in herself. After all she was a detective. She had chosen that profession because it would allow all the hunting instincts to emerge. She liked her job. She liked the skills it demanded. She liked pretending she was an animal in the jungle stalking her prey. Yet watching the four in the kitchen from the doorway she found herself imagining that she was a photographer taking pictures, holding each gesture in still motion so she could take it home and look at it over and over again. As if by looking

In her role as photographer she would call herself Sister Ray. She would be the female hidden rejected side of the male. And naturally the male would be the object of her camera eye.

she could begin to live it, to become what was in the picture and thereby know it from the inside out. The thought amused, thinking of herself as a photographer, thinking of herself in the same role as ManRay whose work she admired. In her role as photographer she would call herself Sister Ray. She would be the female hidden rejected side of the male. And naturally the male would be the object of her camera eye. She would take him apart bit by bit as ManRay had done with various women he had captured, shot, taken photographed. Standing in the doorway Sister Ray imagined herself shooting him as he stood before her talking about women's rights. She moved from angle to angle hoping to capture just the right gesture of insecurity and betrayal, hoping to take that look of utter withdrawal and bring it to the fore, so that it would cover his face like a mask, shielding and protecting him.

It was only when she felt a push against her ribs, an elbow, and caught a glimpse of the first sheet-white woman pushing her through the dark to get out of the door, that it occurred to Ray that she had been staring intently at the four people in front of her—the merry drinking, partying four and she wondered if he had noticed. Every time she looked at him, she looked in such a way that she ceased to be the hunter and became the prey. As Sister Ray she turned to take a photograph of herself. Self-portrait titled "woman in the role of victim." No! she did not like that title "women as prey." No! she did not like that title either. There it came to her in a flash "woman being seduced by the gaze of an unknown man." Black and white self-portrait. And Ray thought what would make the portrait interesting would be the eyes, for they would look as if they were drowning in light and the body would look as if it were naked well almost naked except for the desire draped around it. Anyway he did not seem to be noticing her. He was too busy talking, drinking and searching for a cigarette to smoke. Ray hated smokers. She believed them to be permanently flawed, like some delicate vase broke and glued back together again so well that the crack could not be seen, but occasionally it would fall apart reminding, needing to be glued all over again. It wasn't that she did not think everyone flawed, broke, cracked in some way. It was more that she could not tolerate the way smokers announced it each time they lit a cigarette.

Smelling the smoke mingled with the scent of his noticing her and pretending not to notice her, mingled with the desire she felt and the fear that it would not be satisfied, Ray became nauseous. She felt it both ways as an extreme disgust for the man standing in front of her, as a sickness overcoming her so that she had to rush past the group with her hand covering her mouth and searching for the nearest bathroom. She could hear them laughing and yelling as she made her way upstairs. Upstairs she was able to vomit in peace. To get down on her knees before the toilet bowl and retch again and again. She had always hated vomiting and struggled to suppress any need to vomit no "throw up" that was what they called it as children. It was when she learned to menstruate that she began to throw up regularly once a month. It was her fantasy that if the bloody discharge coupled with all the pain and discomfort it caused (not to mention the moments of embarrassment and shame) were to be thrown up out of the mouth instead of the vagina it would be so much easier to accept. After throwing up she would usually sit on the cold floor of the bathroom and weep wildly as though she had endured some intense torture. After the weeping she would feel a peace as intense as the pain had been. This time during the moment of peace she began to giggle thinking about how like high school it all was, her longing to attract his attention, to get him to notice her and she finally gets his attention in a way that is nothing like the look of desire. It was all disgust.

She walked down the stairs with an amused look on her face. This time staring straight at her and said, "Here we have an expert on women's rights, after all she is a woman doing a man's job or so I've heard. Let's ask her what she thinks about equal rights." Although she had been listening to their conversation all the while as she stood in the doorway, she had not listened well enough to know what they were really saying.

She had been too busy recording other things. Staring at him Ray said she didn't really come to parties to discuss politics, that in fact she didn't like parties or discussions at parties. She turned to walk away confident that the challenging look in his eyes revealed that he not only noticed her but had been waiting for the moment when he could push her up against the wall, or she thought pin her to a wall, covered with dead and captured butterflies. Yes, she was absolutely sure that he had been one of those little brute boys who liked to tear things apart, kill them in front of your very eyes just to see the terror take over one's face. Still it was also clear that he had not been ready for the swift and cutting response, or the way she stood there next to him and the group not saying a word, watching him alternatively with a face blank and indifferent—with a face terrorized and excited by desire.

She had been standing too long, too rigid in the same position bemused by her own wanderings while the party people had begun to move on.

She was back to thinking about photography only this time not about ManRay but about the photographer who managed to capture in her photos something of the horror in ourselves and our daily lives. Like so many other people, she had not liked many of the photographs taken by Diane Arbus especially the ones of the truly different-in-body people, the giant, the midget. Ray always managed to open photography books in stores and swiftly turn her eyes away from the Arbus photographs. When she looked at an entire book of these photographs it hurt. She could feel her heart being attacked by sorrow, the pages by tears—photographs wet by tears. She wondered how she would look now if Arbus were standing in front of her—shooting straight, capturing the horror and the excitement in the moment of seduction which is also like the moment of murder. Ray changed her mind. Arbus would not be the right photographer for the moment. For she would expose too much of the stark horror of it all.

No Ray would go back more than a few years and hire that fine black photographer James Van Der Zee. He had a way of photographing horror so that it appeared seductive and sweet, so that it showed all the complexity of the thing. Ray was standing there with one ear hearing that the party conversation was going on about her remembering the one photograph of Van Der Zee's she could always see with her eyes closed, the one of the wedding. Van Der Zee often took photographs of those everyday human rituals as a way to make a living but this one was special for just as he prepares to take a picture of the bride she is shot by a secret lover. As the crowd holds her dying they implore her to say his name. She is silent. Perhaps it is too much to read into a photograph but Van Der Zee seemed to always tell the truth, the whole truth, and nothing but the truth, so entire stories could be heard pouring forth from his photographs. Perhaps that was the link between him and Arbus. So Ray if she could, if she had the power to bring them back from the dead would do so. She'd ask them both to take a photo and then stick the prints somewhere on a wall next to each other to hear the slightly different stories they would tell.

Her leg had gone to sleep. She had been standing too long, too rigid in the same position bemused by her own wanderings while the party people had begun to move on. As he walked past her, she was able to ask in her best voice for such occasions clear like a crystal, like a bell ringing but very very seductive that he wait a moment. She wondered if he felt that the hands clutching his arms were really a handcuff, that she was really arresting him. She said it straight—"I like to eat lunch, it's my favorite meal, will you join me sometime."

She said it all straight but very fast. She was a fast talker. Her voice moved like a racing car. He said, "why not, I'd like that." He agreed so quickly, so without thought that Ray was taken back. So she said "okay sometime." It was him that said, "why not make a time now." And she did. She suggested Wednesday for growing up it had been her favorite day—the day for prayer meeting, and choir practice. She had loved sitting in the cold basement of the church singing. She was always moved by the warmth of the voices and the songs—carried away so completely that she would not even notice the still agony expressed in the quiet prayers, the long-winded prayers of the deacons. So Wednesday it would be. She told him to meet her at Leila's knowing all the time that he would not know what it was, where it was. It was her time to challenge him. It was a funky soul food place hidden away on a dead-end street, at the very very end of a neighborhood. "You know," she said, "the kind of neighborhood some of us grew up in."

After they agreed to meet, he went back to his phony lying self—the one that had been talking and partying all evening; the one she had quietly grown to hate all through the years of knowing who he was, watching him but never speaking to him. He needed to go back to his party. That's right, Ray remembered. It was his birthday. She said, "happy birthday" to his back knowing all the time that it meant nothing to him, because birthdays didn't mean anything how could they for someone not growing up. Their encounter had left Ray feeling exhausted tired and just a bit peeved with herself. She was glad that the party was in the other room. She was glad to have the kitchen all to herself. Only she did not keep standing. She hated standing, maybe that was one of the reasons she found parties so difficult. She liked to talk sitting not standing. She sat at the kitchen table by herself listening to the music, thinking about the nature of sexuality and desire. She had danced a couple of times with people she did not know. Another thing she did not like about parties. In a culture where nobody hardly ever touched any other body that it did not know, suddenly you could be somewhere dancing with a stranger feeling his body and smelling his breath and having his arms hold you tighter than you wanted to be held. Of course sometimes it was arousing this moment of intimacy with a stranger. But most times it was just disgusting. Ray always broke away in the middle of the dance, always claimed she was tired. Her partner would always be annoyed, sometimes even hostile. She would walk away anyway ignoring him. People were often shocked that she would dance with a willing woman friend at the terribly heterosexual parties. She had asked herself if she was trying to show off. Black folks can get really annoyed by people trying to show off. But no Ray did it because it did not make sense to her, this world of pressing one's body close to strange men when there were familiar women, someone she would know and shared things. It was better dancing with known bodies. When they decided that she was not showing off they would speculate about the nature of her sexuality. She did not care about that. Anyhow she did not let herself think too much about them and that was a way of hoping they never thought about her.

The kitchen here in this house, lived in by a woman friend and a group of other people whom she only slightly knew, was rather cold. It reminded her of the woman, Lulu the woman she knew better. They had spent time together, talking about clothes, about their love affairs. Lulu had been involved with one man but would not tell Ray his name. This upset Ray's notion of friendship. When she wanted to know why the man could not be named, Lulu simply told her that she did not want to know all the little details. It amazed Ray that Lulu simply assumed she would know details when she wasn't sure she knew many Lulu knew. The secrecy was all too close, too much like a cover-up. That meant of course that she had to know the man, or know of him. Ray had this way of finding out stupid, crazy, insignificant yet very personal details about people she did not know, would not want to know, would never meet. But she had met him she was sure of it now. Just as she was sure that it was he and the woman who had demanded secrecy, who had demanded that Lulu no tell Ray.

It was hard to be friends with a woman who would let someone else tell her what to do, especially this man who was sure to be coming and going in the night like a thief or burglar, who would never really linger in anyone's heart. It took only a little thought, a little work at putting the pieces of the puzzle together for Ray to see him. And if in her role of photographer she had taken a picture of him it would have been out at the local landfill, the dump, wearing his favorite blue jeans, faded of course and a manly looking shirt preferably red plaid, flannel, open at the neck. She would shoot him there standing on a mound of garbage. It was Arbus who suggested that a photographer could capture the soul of a person, that this was the reason photography is both mysterious and sinister. This would be one photograph Ray would not let tell its own story. She would want people to see the unity between him and the garbage. That was of course was not how Arbus would have taken the photograph. She would do it without the garbage but it would be there in his eyes, coming out of his pockets, smelling rotten and stinking up the photograph. Yes an Arbus photograph would do all that without the garbage, that of course was why Arbus was the photographer and Ray a detective. She had the skill only of her eyes and five senses and no camera. In real life she hated taking pictures. Of course in her role as detective she was daily examining photographers, going back to the scene of the crime, that's what the photographers allowed her to do. To tell the truth and nothing but the whole truth. Ray was primarily interested in portraits. She certainly did not give a damn for photographs of landscapes. It was the taking of the portrait that was like seduction. She was interested in seduction.

Seduction had been the need driving her to come to this party when she hated parties. It was amusing. The first time she had seen and met him, it had been at a party, only a party that was a little more bearable. There was no music, no dancing, no hard liquor. It was a book party introducing someone's latest book of poems. Everyone at the party was black and the poet (another woman) set huddled in her chair as if it was raining, as if she was drenched and had been waiting for hours at a lonely and isolated bus stop. She looked cold and frozen. Nothing at all like the robust picture appearing on the back cover. Ray could not stand pictures of the author on book covers. She preferred that the writer be as anonymous as possible, without a face. She preferred to read the words in the book and not get stuck on searching for the story in the portrait on the back. Sometimes if a picture was there she would hold a book a long time staring at the author. Really it was a distraction not something worthy of hatred.

She had the skill only of her eyes and five senses and no camera. In real life she hated taking pictures.

Ray had come to the party with Lulu. The two of them had sat on the couch talking only to one another giggling like girls, like the girl she was never allowed to be. She would not have been caught dead giggling in third, fourth grade, in any grade, but she was doing it now. Somehow the giggles contrasted sharply with the low cut cotton blouse she was wearing. It was a blouse a woman would wear when she wanted to be sexy, alluring, when she wanted to attract attention. Ray wore it for old times' sake, for those were just the reasons she had bought it only to abandon it when she considered herself no longer foolish enough to indulge in such obvious hints. Yet she had worn it this night with a silk skirt. The man, the one she was now longing to be with in the act of seduction, had sat down in front of them only because they were sitting near the food. They were facing each other over a long narrow table. The man was an enemy of Lulu's. Ray had forgotten the story but intended to piece it together later. Because they were enemies Lulu made no move to introduce her. She introduced herself.

He spoke with a West Indian accent. His voice delighted and amused her. It was like a secret for it told her nothing about him, only that he had maybe lived somewhere else, only that he had been brought up by parents who lived somewhere else, maybe by no parents, maybe he had been raised by strangers. Actually what Ray detected even though he only said a few silly sentences to Lulu was that the accent was not really his primary speaking voice at all. It was what Ray would call the voice of memory, somewhere he had spoken it, somewhere it had been truly his but no more. He said nothing to her. She ignored his indifference. She didn't like being around me or any man who was trying to get her attention, trying to get her to notice him. On a second thought Ray realized as he reached for a cigarette that it was not indifference, that in fact he was trying to control an intense and horrific hostility. The secret was whether or not it was directed at Ray, Lulu or all women. He certainly felt hostile towards Lulu and yes Ray thought if murder was not a crime, he would kill Lulu and go on his way like people crush ants or smash flies with books and newspapers.

Ray did not want him to say anything to her. She liked being invisible. It was easier that way to study the person, to draw one's own portrait. In her sketch of him she wrote down at the top of her notebook his name "Beau St. Clair, young very young," she wrote, "maybe not even out of diapers," not she thought "definitely out of diapers, potty trained though sometimes makes mistakes, even walking and talking." Well she put the age at five years old, next to the five she put twenty something and by it a question mark. After his age she wrote, "nice eyes, not at all beautiful just downright dreamy and sexy." Lulu laughed and whispered, "sexy my ass, look like a drunk or a drug addict." In her own way Lulu was good at sizing people up but she always failed to get the whole picture. She only looked at them in relationship to her feelings about them and that Ray thought was a very very dangerous way of looking. Yet still she felt she would learn something by listening to Lulu. She asked her whether or not St. Clair as she began to call him, really was a drunk, a drug addict. It amused Lulu that she called him St. Clair for he really was her embodiment of the devil, everything she feared and despised in men. Yet, if murder had not been a crime, Lulu would have killed him too, not instantly; she would have tortured him in every way imaginable. This kind of intense feeling Ray thought dangerous and sinister because it did not allow for the possibility in any way that what one was seeing when you looked at another person was not them but just someway you wanted them to be, or made them be because it was easier. In that sense the act of murder is taking place all the time, the person's real identity is suffocated by the identity pushed and projected onto them. Sitting with the two of them Ray felt that she was a witness to two equally bizarre crimes for neither person knew who it really was that they were killing.

Hadn't they learned from TV westerns that it was important to know who you were killing, to meet face to face the very life you would take if you were quicker, faster, the fastest gun in the west. Ray had dreamed of growing up to be the fastest gun in the west. As a child she was only allowed to carry one gun—as two guns were not lady like. She did not care. It was better to have one gun than no gun at all. She would stand before the mirror practicing for hours, aiming at the heart, shooting straight. Instinctively, she felt that neither one of these two knew who they were willing to kill. It was something inside themselves something fierce and hidden. If they could annihilate each other they could destroy that something. They would never have to feel it or face it again. It had something to do with blackness, the skin that joined each of them sitting in the room. ■

MESS HALL IN RURAL INDIA

The used banana leaves take attendance here, for the hundreds of fractured faces that flow from the fields through these open doors at noon, and sit pretzeled, hungry and waiting to be served before a large, veined banana leaf.

Leaf-plates collect in the compost heap every afternoon at two, when men and women with toothless smiles and arthritic hands crowd around the washbasins to scrub the beetroot stains from their fingernails.

Still wet with edible finger paint, the green canvases lie, yoghurt white, mango pickle red, turmeric yellow, streaked in thick bands, the width of a fidgeting finger that chaotically crosshatched the canvas, stippled with grains of lemon rice for contrast.

Each leafy canvas is a fingerprint
Each drying design, a new identity.

Behind these doors, poor laborers who come for a free noon meal, who seek respite from sunburned fields of rice,

become artists.

DIVYA RAMESH

THE FINISHER BARN

JESSI LEWIS

We were seven men in dusted T-shirts standing in a flat horizon of layered dead turkeys. When we stepped, their organs crushed under our boots and spread soft and thick. At one time, there had been eight of us in total, all almost-college-graduates. Stan, in the years before we all grew up, before we dropped out of the agriculture program right when we learned how to castrate turkeys, and before he died, led us to all agree on one thing—nobody needs a degree to house birds.

But that was something to argue considering Henry's barn on a spring day when the temperature was starting to rise. Nearly 20,000 turkey carcasses sprawled in the long landscape of the finisher barn, just spoiling away. The corpses were anywhere from one body to three bodies deep, so at times it felt like we were wading through the barn. Henry gave us facemasks to breathe through because the Virginia spring was about to cook the asphyxiated birds. The barn was an oven. We stood in piles of immature roasts.

Pieces of straw sticking up played in the wind of eight fans that made up the back wall of the barn. The sunlight slipping through was broken by each spinning blade. These were the circulation fans that turned off the night before, and, because of some electrical short, the alarm didn't sound to wake Henry up from his dusty cubby in the back. He told us that he couldn't understand it—he slept deeper that night than any other night, like he found comfort in the absence of the fan noise. When he told us this, he looked up at the roof of the barn as though he might cry. The fans, spinning again, looked down on him with no shame at all.

The scene looked as though each bird gave up her life with one final, unnatural embrace of another.

It's easiest to keep the mind off of it, so we started pushing the bodies around with our brooms. We'd add more to the heap in the center of the barn, drop the bodies down, then push the broom over them to turn their heads if they eyed us.

Being together in Henry's barn connected distant memories of a cheap white apartment with hunting arrows stuck in the plaster of the walls. At the time, most of us commuted from our parents' places to go to college classes. But Stan and Henry had a two-bedroom apartment, and they didn't care about the security deposit. That was where we used to play liquor flip cup in the kitchen and shoot bottle rockets down the hall.

We all had cowboy boots in those days. We each had a girl one weekend, before being lonely the next. We'd crash in open spaces on the cold floor of Stan and Henry's place—our base. Once or twice it was all of us together, invading on a weekend, their bathroom smelling like excess spray cologne and the cloud left over the toilet after breakfast.

Once we left college, even though we all learned to help each other out, we stopped caring nearly as much. Some of us got farms and some of us were hired as turkey help. Eventually, we didn't all get together except when there was a hog roast, or when one of us died. There was only one loss so far, and that was Stanley, whose birds didn't last long either.

In school he was the one who introduced us to our wives and ice luge shots. There was some kind of energy in the back of his voice that made us all want to hear him talk, even when he talked shit. Before Henry's birds died, Stan's funeral was the last time we were all together. He had a rocky marriage with a wife who took the battery out of the truck on Saturdays when he'd likely drive while intoxicated, but they loved each other enough for her to wear black and blink a little bit during the minister's talk. Henry couldn't focus on anything during the whole funeral, his eyes wandering.

He had a hard time with it even when everybody else had moved on.

■ ■ ■

While most of us started to sweep up the bodies, Henry went over to test the alarm. The rest of us were starting to feel sweat drops from our hairlines to our collarbones. The red light above the box turned glared to life as he worked on the alarm, but there was no blaring sound. We heard him curse at the fuse box, and then say to the barn, "Stan, what the hell do I do now?"

He and Stan used to drive around town in Stan's boosted truck and yell at girls. Henry was the underweight boy from Buffalo Gap who couldn't get through English, couldn't bring himself to read Melville. It was Stan who let him copy a few papers here and there. It was Stan who helped him raise this barn when Henry dropped out. Stan even came over and watched the turkeys when Henry's lady threatened to leave him if he didn't take a weekend away from the farm. None of us had that same feeling of dependency on each other. There came a point when we avoided calling each other, just focused on work.

Stan had been the one who convinced us that turkeys were the investment of the decade.

He said it so smooth: "A bird farm is shit to dive into and then crawl out of clean and rich."

None of us had the same feeling of dependency on each other. There came a point when we avoided calling each other, just focused on work.

But this wasn't true. Christmas morning was spent in the turkey barn. Easter Sunday, we couldn't escape, even to the last resort of Church. We'd lose some turkeys here and there, we'd spend the income, we'd lose our savings. The comfort that we had in college had left out a side door. Nobody even really realized it was missing until Stan died and we watched Henry fall to pieces at the wake—tears falling into his banana cream pie from the buffet table.

So, the time we took that day at Henry's farm felt weighty and valuable. And all we could really give him was our hands at work.

The brooms kept pushing along.

One of us said, "We need a lot of pennies for these little eyes," but it wasn't as funny as it should have been. We moved for two hours more and just didn't talk.

Then Henry started yelling too loud while calling up the high school kid who helped out at the farm.

"You come here last night, you little shit?—You fuck with the alarm?"

Henry spit as he spoke. We listened, all of us wishing Stanley was there.

It was clear the way we moved around each other, making little comments about the bird shit at our toes, Stan's vacant spot was still there. There was a space, always a space, where Stanley would have stood, usually on the right, sometimes in the center. He would have had cigarettes rolled up in his sleeve. He would have looked like a heartthrob from the 1960s with his hair slicked back and his wide chin.

While turkeys piled up in the middle of our movements, awkward, scaly legs stuck out this way and that. We began to get used to the smell of them, and even the dust. When one of the turkeys dropped from a height or rolled off the top of the pile, it would leave a comet's trail through the thick barn air.

When Henry finally got off the phone, he came back to help us. It was easier to focus on the grit in our socks than to look at him. He looked around at us with a couple turns of his head, tears in a sheen, then went to get the truck to cover up the fact that he was gasping. He and Stan built a garage door into one panel in the long barn. This is where he pulled the truck through. We started with shovels—some longer handled digging shovels, a fox shovel, a snow shovel even—and we tossed small bodies of the birds into the bed of the truck. The pile we had would easily fill the back of Henry's truck, and there were still double, maybe quadruple the number of birds waiting to be moved from the place where they collapsed.

We paused when we heard movement—scrapes of rough, clawed feet in the bottom of the truck. The sounds continued. We gathered around the bed of the truck with our shoulders touching.

The pile of bird bodies in the bed smelled so strong, our lungs closed up again instinctively. Feathers started stirring.

There was a live bird.

Its dry, pink head appeared first as it crawled out from under six others. The thing was broken to pieces, and pulled itself along with one leg missing. Somebody's shovel had cut it clean through. We watched the wounded bird move toward the back of the truck bed and squawk feebly. We tried to pretend it wasn't horrible—the look of that broken leg as she climbed out from the remains of her village.

Henry said, "Oh, Jesus Christ."

Someone else said, "How the hell is she still going?"

Stan came into our minds again when Henry said, "Let's put her out of her misery," because that's what Stan would have done. He shot his dog for snapping at his kids. He killed the turkeys that looked too sick to get on the truck and go to the company, even when the company men would accept them. And he could always swiftly and logically explain his choices. It was the same conversation you might have with a man who returned his table saw to the store. He'd stand there and explain with his hands in his pockets. Only his thumbs would stick out.

But we weren't all that much like Stan. Nobody moved to kill the bird. Nobody picked up their shovel. The turkey stood up on one leg and turned to look at us. She spun around a bit and lifted her wobbly little wings. It looked for a moment like a dance. She was the last tragic ballerina on just one pointed leg. Henry finally walked over to the twirling turkey, picked her up and put her on the ground by his feet. Most of us turned away when he stepped on her head.

The truth is, we should have been used to this by now. We should have known that you're always haunted by the turkeys that never made it back onto the trucks, and that Henry's bitterness made sense. He wasn't the only one who lost birds, and he certainly didn't hold the record of losses among us. When Stan died, it wasn't the first time he lost a flock.

He hung himself from a ceiling beam on a morning when his alarm was going off, the fans were dead and the turkeys were too.

He, like the rest of us, was only partially in control since the company brought him the birds' food and antibiotics. It was the company that designed the birds to be abnormal. Even how they walked wasn't really like turkeys were meant to be. But this time, for Stan, the birds didn't catch a sickness, they didn't get picked off hundreds at a time by the coyotes and foxes. Even the warning system worked when the fans turned off, but Stan was too drunk to wake up in time to save his birds.

When it came down to it, Stan was the reason that the birds croaked, and so he did what only Stan would do—kill the animal with the flaw. His wife found him swinging by an electrical cord. He knew she would find him there when she came looking for him right after dark.

It was probably a relief for her when Stan kicked the bucket. She and her kids could leave the barns behind and move in with her parents. Stan was a charming man, but he was a problem-husband. He walked with steps too wide, a flask always halfway open. He called out at ladies on the other side of the street downtown even when it was four in the afternoon, even though he was too old to do that anymore.

We all heard about Ron's sister.

At this time she was fourteen, and Stan saw her on Main Street in town and called out to her, "Jesus Christ, baby, I could roll you in jelly."

And she said back, "Stan Farris?"

We all took two steps away from Stan.

But Henry didn't let all of this bother him. He and Stan laughed about yelling at Ron's sister—a classic mistake.

Henry was not Stan, but he wanted to be. He looked down at that dead turkey under his foot, the bones of her head splayed.

We shook our heads and the shoveling started again.

More clawing sounds.

At this we stopped again. The birds were dead, they had been dead all morning, but three more rose up like little odd phoenix. This time, all three were whole, which was even odder, since the shovels we were using were sharp enough to sometimes cut through whole turkey. These birds came up like the first—slow, and then faster with the oxygen reaching them. The feathers of their families fell away.

The birds were dead, they had been dead all morning, but three more rose up like little odd phoenix.

We all had a second of thought before Ron, Allen and I each grabbed a bird at the neck before Henry could argue. Henry followed as we all walked the three turkeys out the garage door, over the gravel, and let them go in Henry's field. The birds wandered around the empty land, the yellow of the sunlight tossing over their feathers. Their distant looks were a reminder that we weren't college kids anymore getting prepared to live off the fat of the land, to take advantage of what God gave us. We weren't working to bring the finest materials to American dinner tables. These birds weren't really birds anymore.

They didn't have that buried instinct to run and love the ground under their feet, to find an escape route, to hunker in the woods and wait for us to give up on our search.

Instead, they walked around each other.

They looked at us.

One sat down on the ground with her feet scraping the dirt.

We left the birds there and got back to work. Henry was a little annoyed that we chose life over death, but he didn't mind so much if it meant we'd keep working. He looked at the birds, pushed his feet around in the gravel of the front yard and then got back to it.

The scrape of our shovels formed a beat that continued for a half hour or so. The sun's angle changed and our shadows moved with it. Henry was the first to look back outside. He cried out loud, and sat, his ass in the garage doorway. A half gasp came out of him. It took us all a second to see what it was he was looking at. Shane, who was always concerned about hearts, knelt next to Henry, thinking that maybe he needed some aspirin to thin his blood. Maybe he was getting backed up with the pressure rolling from his emotions. Damned up tears.

The birds stood out in the field together in a line, the tallest of them in the center. Their shadows swept over the gravel.

"Jesus Christ," somebody said.

Most of us choked on our own throats.

The turkeys outside were dancing.

They slowly began to spin. As they spun in unison, they each dragged one foot in an arc around themselves. It was hard for any of us to really consider it a dance at first because they squawked regularly, looking confused, and their eyes only moved from each other to us, and then back to each other. But there wasn't any other way to describe it. The dance seemed organized; it seemed purposeful somehow.

We sat down in the gravel outside the garage door and watched as though we had paid the ticket fees. The gravel bit through our jeans and the sun turned on to broil, but we sat anyway. We fell in rows—all seven of us—with an empty space for Stan on the right side. Allen had a hand over his mouth while Ed and Ron looked from the birds back to the sky regularly. Shane traced his thumbnail on his knee as he watched. Alec sat cross-legged, confused and I sat next to him, shaking my head too many times. Henry hunkered next to me. We were in two rows, our steel toe boots dusty.

During the show, it was suddenly clear that Stan was not actually with us—his spirit could not be wandering between us in any way, even though we left him some space to do so. He would never let those turkeys dance in the gravel like humanly, feathery puffs.

Henry's tears rolled out over his dirty cheeks stained already with caramel sweat streaks. We nodded at him at different times during the performance, trying to say in a couple glances that it's just fine, it's all right.

We looked back at the odd group of birds dancing slowly, rotating. They were like people—dancers in a musical prepping for the most important scene, the little girls in dance studios standing in front of mirrors. The turkeys went on for twenty minutes until they started to weaken. Eventually they died. Their bodies lowered down to the border between gravel and grass. Their little eyes, actually, shockingly, closed.

This was somehow too odd an event for all of us to keep on working. We came as a favor to Henry, and partially as a favor to the late Stan, but the birds changed everything. They rearranged our fingers and left singed marks in our thoughts.

Henry tried to go out and squash the heads of the bird bodies out in the gravel, but we stopped him.

We ran our hands over our foreheads. The wrinkles around our eyebrows deepened. We wondered how it was that we could see the dancing turkeys so clearly while Henry seemed to see something else entirely. He couldn't tell that they had breathed at one time, squawked in surprise and leaned on each other.

It was supposed to be our job to help him fill the Stanley-hole, guide Henry to the information on his contract, keep on shoveling bird bodies all day and into the night under the long rows of lights in the barn while our hired boys were back home taking care of our own turkeys. But what we were supposed to do suddenly seemed to get a little too distant from what was actually happening. After the turkeys danced, we didn't even know what to do with our hands, if they were supposed to be out in the air or deep in our pockets.

We ran our hands over our foreheads. The wrinkles around our eyebrows deepened.

Some of us inspected the bodies of the birds in the sunlight. Poked at their awkward legs. Pushed their heads around to face the barn.

The rest of us looked at those dancing birds from a few feet away while we smoked cigarettes. For a good half hour, we were silent. Henry got up and went back inside to keep shoveling turkeys. The little pieces of Stan that Henry had adopted showed in his work. We could hear the scrape of his shovel on the floor of the barn.

Some of us followed Henry into the barn. We finished filling the truck and then moved on to piling the next stack of turkeys. There were no sounds of birds rising up from their layers. None came up for air. The show was over.

But some of us didn't go back to work right away. Ed and Shane called their wives instead and told them what happened with the turkey dance. Those of us working shook our heads at those two as they paced around the gravel and looked for the best signal. An hour later, they came back into the barn to help us finish it.

But even as some of us worked and some of us called wives, there were two who didn't join in to do either. Ron and Allen left for the row of trucks and SUV's parked up the road, the color of their jeans and T-shirts wavering in the heat. With a last line of, "To hell with this," they were gone. We called from the barn and they called something back—inaudible stretched words that let the vowels and consonants glide together. Their tires kicked up mud. The brake lights didn't come on because neither of them wanted to use their brakes.

■ ■ ■

Ron and Allen didn't raise turkeys the following year, and never came back to Henry's farm, any hog roast or funeral.

We never stood in a finishing barn together again—all seven of us. Some of us had predicted this in a way, but we had bet that middle age would be the thing that caused the sudden break. Instead it was dusty, dancing turkeys.

■ ■ ■

With the barn finally cleared out around one in the morning and all of us left by two, Henry purposefully forgot about the bodies of the turkeys outside and he ignored the sound of dogs on the road when he fell asleep. These were two stray hounds that slipped into the field from the woods with the wet, soft sound of their paws in the mud, and then the drag of their back feet in the gravel as they came to a sudden halt. With the bodies of the dancing turkeys in their mouths, they jumped the fence and tore off into the line of haggard cedars and maples on the edge of the field. Henry noticed a trail of feathers in the morning, and he thought about picking up each one as though to save them. Then he remembered that they were just food birds anyway, bred to have feathers of no value at all.

Henry didn't kill himself, even though the wives that were called on the day of the bird dance predicted that he would. Instead, he got the electrical short in the fans fixed and then ordered another batch of turkeys. It was as though this time there would be no dance, just profit. He took out a loan he couldn't afford just to keep going. His temperamental wife had a temperamental baby with chubby fat around its neck and waist. They named the child Stanley without really thinking about the dancing turkeys and what it meant to stand outside of the barn for a moment before dying. ■

AFTERMATH

for my brother

You witness an explosion
you calculate in numbers
so small their heat shatters
into white flame. Subatomic
heartbreak rolls into the clouds.

A star the reaction lit
like a candle snaps in blue
above the microscopic field
of your narrowing choices.

Here, floating above the blast
a black thread frays, widens
in the nuclear wind
like the shadow of a man
risen from the fracture.

MARCIA L. HURLOW

PRODIGAL

1. Recklessly wasteful; 2. Lavishly generous.

He's embarrassed by the plums
of this place, the way they fall
in sticky lushness, their endless bearing
judgment on his competence, his failure
to find their use. He doesn't hail
from a barren place. Back home oaks
and poplars race for the sky, kudzu fastens
tendrils and buries alive anything
that hasn't mastered being fast.

But this black soil boils with seed
and birth. The neighbors beg
anyone to take apricots, oranges,
peaches that melt to slick slime
on the brittle grass. What can be done
with the too-muchness of this world,
but to bow like a tree encumbered
by blessings, like a psalmist whose cup
flows to perplexing excess.

JANE SASSER

WHAT SHE HADN'T KNOWN

I'd like to apologize for the loose cows of my childhood,
the ones who wandered the roads at two a. m., lowing
as if to say, *how did such a thing happen? How*
did we find ourselves in your garden, cropping
the corn? I'm sorry for our stretched-out fence,
for their eagerness to test the old cliché, for the shock
of a face at your window, bovine and large, stuff
no one's dreams are made of. I'd like to apologize
if I moved a little too slowly to herd them home,
watching the way five hundred pounds could frolic,
their tails like banners in air, proclaiming *this pasture*
of the world is ours, this grass the sweetest
we've ever known, this range the freest pass
to paradise brute beast could ever crave.

JANE SASSER

THE CURVE OF THE SMOKE

BETH NEWBERRY

On a Thursday night in late June, the air is sticky on my skin as I smoke a cigarette at my kitchen window and watch the smoke curl into the air. It curves like my fingers do when I hold a pen. I stand at the open window and face the butter-colored aluminum siding of the building next to mine. I smoke a cigarette because I want one even though it doesn't provide the buzz or sensation of relief that I expect. The Marlboro Light rests just where a pen does—between the callus on my middle finger and the tip of my index finger. I look at my fingertips and then past my hand to the snail-shell-shaped circles of pigeon excrement on the paint-chipped windowsill.

My cell phone rings and I stretch to reach it on the edge of the countertop as I try unsuccessfully to keep the cigarette smoke outside of the window. "Bethie," my friend Alan cajoles. "Let's go out." The final word out has several symbols, as Alan expands the three letters with significant whining. I turn him down.

"I have to write," I say.

"Just one drink. You'll be home by midnight."

I think it over briefly as I consider my cigarette: Date with my friend, or date with my cigarette. "Can't do it. How about tomorrow. After work?"

I feel guilty as I end the call. And then I think, It's okay. I'll get the smoking out of my system tonight and go smoke-free tomorrow. Alan thinks I have quit. I thought I had quit, too. But I switched my social smoking habit for a private one. A habit-inducing trade off. I feel guilty for lying by omission, for stinking up my apartment, and for blatantly flaunting a disregard for the Surgeon General warnings about cancer, emphysema and the eternal damnation that smoking causes.

I stand and think about the view from the front windows of my apartment, the activity of the sidewalk below: I'm not observing any of it at the moment, all I can see is the siding on the second story of the building next to mine that houses a Japanese restaurant. I close my eyes and listen to the sounds of customers talking on the restaurant's patio, the bass line of the acid jazz music from the speakers, and the shifting of gears and acceleration of a car at the traffic light. I smell seaweed and sesame oil and exhaust and the ripeness of the summer heat.

I inhale a final drag and put out the cherry of the cigarette, like a miniature harvest moon disappearing in the horizon of chipped paint on the sill. I breathe out slowly and walk from the kitchen at the rear of my apartment to my desk, facing the street. I make my hands move across the keyboard before I can fully realize the cigarette is gone.

■ ■ ■

On Friday morning, the half-full pack sits on the kitchen counter as I head to the coffee pot. I go to throw the cigarettes away, but put them in my purse instead. I feel a slight pain behind my rib, like the corroding of my lungs has deepened a layer.

I don't want to be a smoker, I think. I'm standing at my kitchen counter, adjacent to the smoking window. I've emptied the contents of my purse from the evening before: bar receipt, cigarettes, lighter, wallet, gum, and lip balm.

A month ago, I started graduate school. A month before that I stopped smoking, and I lost the everyday taste for the cigarette. I stopped salivating when I heard the sound of the lighter. I forgot the satisfaction in the motion of the first drag and the last exhalation. I gladly moved away from the dirty kitchen window speckled with feathers, pigeon poop residue and pollen particles.

So now, a month after the month I quit and relinquished my habit, I am smoking again. But why? It's a habit that calms my racecar-speed thoughts. Smoking busies my hands that want to be near paper, tying letters together into words and creating stories. It's much easier to stand and smoke than sit and write. I think slower—words and observations come together without the judgment I feel at the page.

I open the window and light a cigarette. I light a cigarette and my body feels lighter. I feel guilty. But I don't relinquish my smoke. The cigarette keeps my hands busy the way a pen would. My fingers rest in a similar slope, a natural curve as if it were a pencil I lifted from the page. My fingers rest around the cigarette in a shadow of a fist just as they might perch above a keyboard when I'm in mid-thought.

■ ■ ■

Sometimes smoking tastes good, providing a sense of satisfaction the way a conversation with a good friend might. The cigarette has flavors that are smoky, like wood or the last swill of a glass of red wine. Other times I feel as if I am breathing in campfire or am coating my mouth with cured bacon. Smoking shouldn't taste like pork.

I really want this cigarette to taste good. Sometimes, with the better smokes, I have a clear distilled thought. Today, I want just one, or if I'm lucky a series of thoughts that will flow into sentences and then build into a paragraph. I am supposed to sit down and write an essay. But for this moment, I sit on the countertop and hold my arm out the kitchen window. I am developing a scene with a cigarette between my fingers instead of a pen. I couldn't have written this at my laptop, only standing at the window, I think.

I look at the cigarette and the fine ribbon of smoke it distills. The orange line at the base of the ash divides past and future, smoked and unsmoked, and the decision to put it out or keep on smoking. Sometimes when I smoke in the kitchen, I will finish the cig half way through or two-thirds through and put it out because I know there are more.

I have rituals for smoking and rituals for trying to forget I smoke. I think habits are more about having small traditions to build my life around. When I smoke out my window I have a full four minutes where I stand still and concentrate on one task, one set of motions, or one thought. And at least in those four minutes I know what it's like to pray, to create clear thoughts, to write easily. I hold still and thoughts float in on my breath and out on my exhalation, curling out the window with the smoke.

I think: This is it. I'm quitting. No more. I smoke this cigarette close to the filter because I have never liked saying goodbye. ■

LUNA MOTH

She has one week to live.

The first night, she appears
at my window: finch-sized,
owl-spotted, swallow-tailed.
Astounding me with her
vivid green beauty.

Mouthless, she is not driven
by ordinary hunger. She craves
moonlight and streetlight, mates
after midnight, leaves legions
of eggs on the underside of
black walnut leaves.

Her caterpillar offspring
will never know her.
After the seventh day,
I find her in the grass,
lime wings faded to celadon
and tattering
in the wind.

KATHLEEN LEWIS

THE POET AT FIFTY-NINE

—after Larry Levis

Autumn is a glum raisin,
plumped with sweet wine,
stirred into a spiced batter.
As the cake bakes, scents rising,
I think of the woman
who taught me to make it,
of everything I learned
from all the old women:
How to seed zinnias and play canasta,
make artichoke relish and ambrosia,
tie French knots, polish the silver,
the hemming and pressing of skirts.

These women spun stories
on the porch in evening,
waiting for the house to cool.
Hung strips of foil on grapevines
so bluejays wouldn't steal the ripe fruit.
Snatched clothes off lines before storms struck,
wrote letters to men at war. They learned to swim
through disappointment in green creeks,
and some spoke, softly, of babies they'd lost.

The first dark has entered the trees,
diminishing their saffron glow.
I've mixed a cocktail, opened a can of almonds
to eat with the warm cake. My thoughts meld
with the murmurings of the old women,

in the dim parlors of memory.
The words go on, a braided rope.
Lessons have been learned.
The grapevines are bare.
The land is mine.

KATHLEEN LEWIS

ASHEBORO, N.C.

I can't hear ghosts
in the covered bridge's walls,
though I let my knuckles

rest awhile on their wood-damp
whisperings, where they were
scratched into almost-permanence

with pens and pocket knives.
Between boards, under moss, in old oak
cracks—they are suspended here

loving each other a way I can't
remember how. Their toes twine
deep into time and dark earth,

arms turn to willow branches
tucked around shoulders,
mouths grow into shapes of names

that meant everything to someone—
syllables that dangle
from weepy fingers, float easy

as wind chimes ring
their tune older than words
anyone can recall.

CONOR SCRUTON

MARY YODER, WALKING

LYDIA MUNNELL

I think of Mary Yoder standing just outside the kitchen door, one foot holding it open, swatting mosquitos in the white flood light. She smoked a cigarette like it was delicious. Her waist-length hair was tied back in a tight ponytail and then braided—she hadn't figured that part out yet. But she knew how to talk, and she talked slow and low and gravel.

She turned her Pennsylvania Dutch into a real deep Dietrich German. When she came to stay with us, she woke up at 5 a.m. and walked up and down the hill until the sun came up. Mom said Mary was used to getting up early. Pop said she had a demon that followed her around, and every morning he sat by her bed and talked and talked and talked until there was no point in trying to sleep anyway. A demon that looked like her daddy.

■ ■ ■

Mom said it's hard being a woman without a family, and I remember saying it back one day—parroting it to them when I got in trouble for this or that and decided to run away. I walked up the hill with a Golden Dawn bag full of clean underwear and a few sticks that looked like they'd make good slingshots. When I got to the top, I saw how small my house looked down at the bottom, how far away. I ran home with a demon of my own behind me. Inside, Mom and Pop were fixing dinner, and they ignored me. But Mary was just inside the door, and she held me and wiped my eyes with her shirt collar. I breathed her in, clean laundry and dish soap. I remember thinking, this is a woman. We were both learning how to be.

■ ■ ■

Mary left her family for an English boy, the one who taught her how to smoke, but Mom told us it didn't work out. Sometimes the phone would ring, and Mom would hand it to Pop, and he'd lower his voice, and he'd say go to hell. Mom would lead us into the next room, and when I'd ask who Pop was talking to and what about, she'd smile and brush my forehead.

Man stuff, she'd say.

And I'd think about the boy as I imagined him—covered in dark light—while I watched Mary pull on her panty hose. And I'd think about how she must be thinking about him too.

■ ■ ■

When Mary got into community college, Pop brought home a bottle of champagne, and he made a ceremony of opening it, singing like Marlene Dietrich singing "I Can't Give You Anything But Love." Mary said her accent—though still far off—was closer than any of ours to her mother's. And she and Mom and Pop stayed up late some nights listening to Marlene and talking. And Mary was penciling her eyebrows thin like Marlene. Learning to be a woman; but otherworldly. When the cork finally came loose, it shot straight into Mom's new dome light, and she cursed, but nobody bothered to fish it out. And we all stayed up late laughing about it, a little dark spot in the light above our table.

■ ■ ■

Work and school kept Mary away long hours, and when she was gone, I'd fish through her things, and I'd smell them one at a time: her hairbrush, her bath towel, her quilt crazed with age. She did not have yearbooks. She did not have photo albums. All I had to study was Mom and Pop and these few, precious artifacts of womanhood. I was in the slow years before my period, and Mary seemed so very perfect. One afternoon, I found a musty handkerchief—a man's—at the back of her sock drawer. I smelled it too. Plunged my face into it and back out like a baptism. I was a devotee. And Mary wasn't fallen yet. At least not to me. But she was going out then, longer and longer.

And she seemed to go deeper and deeper into the night, until she didn't come back at all.

■ ■ ■

Years later, I saw Mary again, and not since. I was home from college for the summer working the night shift at the desk at Howard Johnson's. I was calling my first real boyfriend on my breaks and negotiating my mandatory orange polo shirt and khakis over chest and hips, wearing makeup because a girl in my dorm said I should. Someone ran in from the hotel bar to tell me there was a fight in the parking lot, and I grabbed the cordless phone and walked to the window to have look. Two men were rolling back and forth over the hood of a car, hands swinging viciously, one was wearing khaki shorts and a shirt with French cuffs—a man from somewhere else come in off the highway. The other man was wearing deep blue denim and Brahmas and his hair was dark with grease. And he was swatting, gesturing for someone to stand back. My eyes followed his hands, and I saw a woman with straight hair and feathered bangs. Her body was still taught and tall and, smoking a cigarette, her face a little wrinkled. She was cringing with each swing, her eyes squinted and carefully lined black with makeup. As I dialed the police, I ignored the tugging I felt to get Mary, to ask her inside, to hug her. To see if she still smelled so clean.

■ ■ ■

Now I go for walks, and sometimes I think about the way Mary used to move up and down the hill, in and out of our world like there was someone chasing her. At Mom and Pop's, there's still a shadow in the dome light in the dining room, but

I really don't look up anymore. I am grown, I say. I know who I am, I say. But something about childhood aches, and every time, I allow that pain to chase me out of the house, to follow me for a while. I am a woman now, and there's not a woman in the world who doesn't know the feeling of someone behind her. ■

CALLING OUT THE DEAD

I was a sound sleeper in my teens. My mother's voice
used to break through my dreams, waking me for school with news.
Hey, that funny guy from Saturday Night Live died,

what's his name, Ackroyd? Or, They shot one of the Beatles.
I'm trying to hear her tone again, trying out instruments:
cello? flute? Clarinet, I think, if a clarinet can drawl *Pam*

into three syllables. It's been seven years since she died,
seven minutes after midnight on the day after
my husband's birthday in Aunt Mildred's living room

over the mountain from the creek where Annie Dillard wrote
The whole world sparks and flames. All of us there,
praying, singing, joking. As my perfect nurse cousin Trena

checked her vitals, I sat by the borrowed bed, above my mother's
still head, a plate of casserole on my lap. We listened
to the spaces between breaths. After, as Trena retold it,

she always included *Pam was right there,*
eating macaroni and cheese. Did I sleep that night?
After the undertaker was summoned from down the road,

after he and his son and the gurney had gone, I lay
on Aunt Mildred's hard-pillowed sofa, which still
smelled of the Grand Home Furnishings store, next to

the empty metal bed, its pale sheets gone. *The whole world*
sparks and flames: a bright jitter that nudged me to rise
the next morning, with no broadside to rouse me.

PAMELA MURRAY WINTERS

LOOKING FOR EFFIE

LEATHA KENDRICK

Perhaps the aim on which we placed our mind
Is high, and its attainment slow to find;
Or if we reach the mark that we have set,
We still would seek another, farther yet.
Thus all our youth, our strength, our time go past
Till death upon the threshold stands at last,
And back unto our Maker we must give
The life we spent preparing well to live.
—Effie Waller Smith, "Preparation"

This is a story of an unlikely poetic friendship and its evolution. It's a meditation on the silences of women who write. And it's a mystery—a story of a writer whose works had been almost completely lost to us prior to the 1980s and of the authorship of poems and stories which until quite recently has been hard to confirm. The friendship story begins in Lexington, Kentucky on January 28, 2015, at the induction ceremony for the Kentucky Writers Hall of Fame. That night Wendell Berry would become the first living writer to receive this honor. Berry was the main reason for the crowd that overflowed the large rooms of the hundred-year-old Carnegie library that evening.

I was a writer in a funk as I took my assigned seat in the lovely, high-ceilinged room, January dark pressing against the wavy glass of the huge old windows. Though Berry had been an important teacher and friend during my graduate school years at the University of Kentucky and I count myself among the many whom he has inspired to write and teach, I almost hadn't come to the ceremony at all. Part of me wanted to be there to see him receive this honor while the rest of me was guiltily aware of my long silences as a writer, my own small output of books, and all of the unfinished work I had just spent the last six months moving from two separate home offices into a new space. I could not admit how much I feared that I would never finish another piece of writing. Exhausted from moving, I wondered if my writing was worth the effort.

I made my way between the tight rows of seats and settled in among the other guests, many of them writers I had come to know over the years. Besides Wendell Berry, the inductees for 2015 included Guy Davenport, Elizabeth Hardwick, Jim Wayne Miller, and Hunter S. Thompson—all familiar names—and one writer whose name I did not recognize: Effie Waller Smith. A sweet, youthful face appeared in the portrait of Effie that was unveiled as part of the ceremony. Handsome and serious-looking, "Miss Effie" (as I soon was calling her) exuded a calm sense of self. The dark face and eyes vibrant above her high-collared white dress seemed to contain a suppressed energy.

Effie Waller Smith was in heady company that night. Looking at her portrait and hearing her poem, "Preparation," I was drawn to her, curious about how it was that I had not known her or her work until now. That evening I learned that nearly all Effie's published writing had appeared during a brief, intense period from 1904 to 1909. A few poems and some short stories appeared after this, the last one in 1917. Then Effie, the writer, disappeared. Effie, the woman, however, did not die until 1960. That fact stopped me. I could not follow what the speaker went on to say. I was stuck in the long wordless blank of years after she'd published those few books.

Effie's silence went to the center of my years-long struggle as a writer and woman. Disoriented and silenced for weeks by the upheaval of my recent move, I learned that evening that Effie's silence coincided with her moving away from her beloved hills. Fearing my own silence, I was determined to save her from hers, or at least to prove that she had not really been silenced by circumstance but had only given up on publication as Emily Dickinson had (as many of my woman writer friends—fine writers—have done). I had to know more about her life story and how that intersected with her artistic history. What stopped her writing? How could Effie have come so close to having a national audience for her work only to abandon it? These questions propelled me to search for Effie Waller Smith.

I had no idea that I would end up spending the next seven months pursuing Effie's life story and looking for the poems I hoped she had written and kept to herself over her long life. I had no idea that the gaps in her life story would capture my imagination and eventually obsess me. And I had no idea I would end up discovering that "Preparation," the poem that sparked my first passion for Effie, was not written by Effie Waller Smith, but by a different Effie Smith in Tennessee whose words and life had also largely disappeared. By the time

I made this discovery, however, I had come to love and admire Miss Effie—and to have made peace with the fact that this Effie, "my" Effie, though she did not author much of the work attributed to her, deserves the place she has come to occupy in Kentucky's literary history.

■ ■ ■

Dedication

I bring this little book
Of simple rhymes, and few
With love sincere and pure
To dedicate to you;
You whom I know and love,
You who are my friends
And live among the mountains—
The dear old Cumberlands.
—*The Author, dedicatory poem in* Rhymes of the Cumberland

As her life story unfolded itself to me, I became aware of just how unfitting this obscurity was for a poet who had once written of the yearning 'For an illustrious name,/ For the applause and praise of men,' . . . Even more unfitting is the fact the Effie Waller Smith, who lived to the ripe age of eighty, stopped writing—or in any case, stopped publishing—at the age of thirty-eight.

—*David Deskins. Introduction to* The Collected Works of Effie Waller Smith

The life story of anyone born in 1879 who did not leave journals and letters behind (as Effie apparently did not) must remain mostly lost to us. We can find bare facts: Census data, gravestones, publication records, and legal documents filed in courthouses; but unless we have access to living people who remember our subject, we will have to conjure a life from the meager bits we can gather. At first I wrote to Miss Effie, as if by asking her across the chasm of years I might somehow hear the person behind the poems and the few facts we know of her.

The Miss Effie I sensed felt like a kindred spirit, her poems recalling ones I'd memorized as a child when *The Best Loved Poems of the American People* was a well-worn volume at our house. I identified with her joy in roaming the outdoors, her pleasure in daily events and the appreciation for the people around her expressed in her verses. An intellect at ease with itself and a pious religious impulse particularly mark the youthful poems of her first book, *Songs of the Months.* Who was this woman whose home in Pike County was only forty miles my own home in eastern Kentucky? What had her life been like as a black girl growing up in mostly white Appalachia before the turn of the twentieth century?

Here are the meager bits of Effie's life I discovered. She was born the third child, second daughter, of Frank Waller and Sibbie (Sibel or Sibyl) Ratliff Waller, both former slaves, in the racially mixed community of Chloe Creek in Pike County, Kentucky, on January 6, 1879. She attended Kentucky State Normal School for Colored Persons (now Kentucky State University), as each of her siblings had done before her. She married twice—first to Lyss Cockerell in 1904 and later to Charlie Smith in 1908. Each time the man left her, and she initiated divorce proceedings within a few months, though apparently her divorce from Charlie Smith was not finalized.[1] Census records show that she was living in Pike County with her family on Chloe Creek in 1880 and 1900.[2]

These bare facts have been woven into a life story by writers and researchers, including Alice Kinder, a Pikeville poet and journalist, and David Deskins, historian, author of the Introduction to *The Collected Works of Effie Waller Smith* and former Pike County Clerk. David Deskins's research and writing helped bring Effie Waller Smith to national attention in the late 1980s.[3] The work of Deskins and Kinder, along with articles and papers written by S.C. Hintz, Joellen Wollangk and others who knew Ruth Smith, Effie's adopted daughter, in Wisconsin form the basis of our current understanding of Smith and her life. As far as I can determine, every biography and analysis of her life and work rests on these sources.

Effie's father, Frank Waller, migrated to Pike County from Virginia sometime before 1870 and settled in Chloe Creek. Deskins notes that "[Frank Waller] was very successful in his capacities as a farmer, blacksmith, and businessman who speculated in property and who accumulated a sizable estate by the time of his death. Though not formally educated, he was known to be an effective manager who valued education."[4]

Though it is impossible to know what and how much Frank and Sibbie Waller read, it's clear they knew of and valued nineteenth century literature, as reflected in naming their son Alfred Tennyson Waller.[5] In interviews after Effie's death, Ruth Smith recalled being told that Effie's "parents

1 David Deskins, "Effie Waller Smith: An Echo Within the Hills," *The Kentucky Review*, Vol. VIII, No. 3, (Autumn 1988), 45.

2 1890 Census records were destroyed by a fire at the Commerce Department in Washington, D.C.

3 Bruce Brown, a professor at Pikeville College whose family owned a copy of Songs of the Months, shared Effie Waller's poems with Kinder and Deskins. Brown can be credited with initiating Effie's rescue from obscurity.

4 David Deskins, Introduction to *The Collected Works of Effie Waller Smith*, (Oxford: Oxford University Press), 6.

5 U.S., World War I Draft Registration Cards, 1917-1918 for Alfred Tennyson Waller. www.ancestry.com.

read to her."[6] In this loving and staunchly Methodist home, Effie thrived intellectually, at ease quoting the classics in even the poems she wrote as a young teenager. She grew into a confident young woman who became Pike County's first certified black teacher in the 1890s while still a teenager.[7] Her older siblings, Alfred and Rosa, had paved the way for her at Kentucky State in the years soon after the college was founded in 1886, and Effie did her studies there around 1900-02.

When she finished her course work, Effie is believed to have taught in schools in Kentucky and Tennessee for most of the next sixteen years, though school district records from the time are incomplete. What we know for sure is that from adolescence into middle age she wrote poetry. Her early poems, collected in *Songs of the Months*, reveal a joyous enjoyment of the natural world and an expansive love for family and friends. As a young teacher she took her students out into the hills to learn the plants, trees and birds and was known for singing to her classes. Alice Kinder called her "the Singing Poet of the Cumberlands."[8]

How vulnerable must she have felt in the months after the failure of her marriage?

I suspect Effie Waller's intelligence and spirit impressed people wherever she went. She seems to have been a young woman with many friends, both white and black. But being a talented and ambitious black woman in the midst of Jim Crow segregation could well have put her in danger. Effie's life span (1879-1960) coincided with the height of our nation's sometimes-violent oppression of African Americans in the wake of Reconstruction. This chapter of our history was much on my mind as I began this essay. The night I first heard of

Effie and her writing, the deaths of Michael Brown and Eric Garner—two black men killed by white police officers—still echoed through the news. I wondered at Effie's apparent fearlessness as I listened to the program speaker relate Effie's love of trekking alone through the rugged terrain of the Breaks of the Mountains, a landscape she mentions often in her poetry.

In 1909 Broadway Press published Effie's second book of poems, *Rhymes from the Cumberland*. This New York vanity press had been engaged by a group of Effie's literary admirers to publish her first book, *Songs of the Months*. By the time *Rhymes* came out (likely funded by Effie herself), Effie had suffered losses that would shape her future. Her marriage to Charlie Smith was over by July of 1908. She'd carried a child, borne it and seen it die.[9] The life she had known up until 1909 must have seemed like a dream. How vulnerable she must have felt in the months after the failure of her marriage? A vulnerability compounded by the physical and emotional aftermath of bearing and losing a child. Could she have been thinking of poetry—particularly of publication—in those months? The 1910 Census records show she is no longer in Pike County, Kentucky. Where did she go?

In 1916 Frank Waller died of a sudden heart attack, leaving his widow, Sibbie, without the safeguard of his respected presence in the community. She was alone, Alfred and Rosa having moved away from Pike County.[10] Effie (and possibly

6 Deskins, Introduction, 6.

7 William R. Cummings, "History of the Perry A. Cline High School," *Journal of the Kentucky Negro Educational Association,* Vol. 9, No. 1-2, 49.

8 Alice J. Kinder, "Singing Poet of the Cumberlands," *Appalachian News Express,* Pikeville, Kentucky, June 18, 1980, Section Three, 1, 4.

9 Deskins, Introduction, 21. [I have not found any conclusive evidence of the child, nor have I been able to locate its burial place.]

10 From 1910 on I am able to find Frank Waller in Census Records in Chicago. So far, I have found no records for Rosa Waller past 1900.

Alfred) returned to help her decide what to do. The Waller's relatively sheltered home where Effie's love of life and learning had been formed could no longer protect her from the harsh realities of the world—racial hatred that erupted in murders and lynchings in the United States, as well as the global tensions that would lead to the First World War. Effie had no doubt seen enough violence around her to last a lifetime, including Charlie Smith's murder in 1911. Her ex-husband, lifelong friend and childhood schoolmate, shot and killed by a white girl while he was trying to serve a warrant as a deputy sheriff. Though the death certificate calls the shooting a homicide, six months later a jury returned a verdict of not guilty.[11]

Effie's childhood and young womanhood of roaming the hills, writing poems that mused on the large events her day and celebrated the people of her community, was not destined to unfold into a settled future in the hills she loved. In the wake of the loss of father, child, and husband, Effie turned to her faith to lead her forward. The Metropolitan Holiness Church Association, an offshoot of the Methodist denomination, had "sent canvassers" into eastern Kentucky throughout the early 1900s, and Effie was moved to cast her lot with them.[12] Uprooting her mother and herself, Effie prepared for a move north, nearer Alfred's Chicago home, to assure financial security and physical safety for herself and her mother.

By 1918 or 1919 Effie and her mother Sibbie had sold their holdings and moved to Waukesha, Wisconsin. Perhaps Smith's restless mind and heart would not have allowed her to stay put, no matter what. Perhaps her deep faith and her determination to make her life matter ordained that she would seek something beyond her beloved mountains. At any rate, the 1920 Census finds Effie Waller Smith on the corner of

Grand and Laflin Avenues in Waukesha, with several hundred other Holiness converts in the former Fountain Springs resort that had been purchased by E. L. Harvey as a communal living site for the Metropolitan Church Association (MCA).

Founded by Harvey in Chicago in 1899,[13] this offshoot of the Methodist Church was a part of the Holiness movement espousing progressive values in the early part of the twentieth century.[14] The Holiness movement, "one of the most significant traditions of ethical and social witness in all of Christendom," had strong appeal for those who wanted to live their religious values.[15] Like other Holiness churches, the MCA "placed great stress on emotional display in public worship and ascetic standards in personal behavior."[16] The twin poles of Holiness worship and practice matched the mix of exuberance and seriousness I sensed in Effie's portrait that January night. Effie's poems reveal a woman who felt deeply; her unsettled life course suggests that she just as deeply needed to channel her passions into worship and service. Appalachian feminist scholar Elizabeth Engelhardt notes that

> *[Effie Waller Smith's] poems speak of ambition, bliss, grief, religion, and friendship. She always returns to her particular location in the mountains, her identity as an*

11 Deskins, Introduction, 8.

12 S.C. Hintz, "The Odyssey of Ruth Smith," unpublished thesis, Wisconsin Lutheran Seminary Library, 4-5. http://www.wlsessays.net/node/2609.

13 Frank D. Farrar, History of the Metropolitan Church Association, http://metrochurchassn.com/history2.html

14 *The New International Dictionary of Pentecostal and Charismatic Movements*, eds. Stanley M. Burgess & Eduard M. van der Mass, (Grand Rapids: Zondervan).

15 Donald W. Dayton, "The Holiness Churches: A Significant Ethical Tradition," http://www.religion-online.org/showarticle.asp?title=1862

16 Deborah Vansau McCauley, *Appalachian Mountain Religion: A History*, (Champaign: University of Illinois Press), 273.

African-American Appalachian, and her combination of what she calls "old fashioned" desires with modern life.[17]

Perhaps Effie's move to the Holiness commune in Wisconsin can best be understood as her enacting her "old-fashioned" desire for a pure life, a life also committed to modern ideals such as women's suffrage, racial equality, and pacifism—Progressive ideas championed by the Metropolitan Church Association.

As I considered Effie's disappearance as a poet, I could not help but think of Gerard Manley Hopkins's exuberance and passion and of how his equally strong conscience and religious vocation led him to shun publication. Effie, like Hopkins, may have felt that poetry was not her truest calling. There is an element of religious asceticism in her poetic silence.

■ ■ ■

[Effie Waller Smith's] exploration of one woman's artistic consciousness—her self-named 'genius of the soul . . .'—suggests that she wished readers to acknowledge her and her characters as inseparably Appalachian, black, and gendered."

—Elizabeth Engelhardt

What are the odds of two potential, aspiring world-class authors, each with legitimate claim to the name Effie Smith, writing at the same time about similar subjects with so much otherwise in common, one of which is ignored due to her color (at least we can understand why) while the other remains unknown and unrecognized in her hometown, county, and state even though she had some extremely notable achievements to her credit, not being the same person?

—*David Deskins,*
"Effie Waller Smith: An Echo Within the Hills"

The body of work attributed to Effie Waller Smith includes three books of poems: *Songs of the Months* (1904, Broadway Books); *Rhymes from the Cumberlands* (September, 1909, Broadway Books); and *Rosemary and Pansies* (December, 1909, Gorham Books, Boston). In addition, David Deskins discovered a few poems and three short stories published by Effie Smith in national journals, including Putnams and Harpers. It seems odd that the second and third books would appear almost simultaneously—in September and December of 1909. There is also a discrepancy in copyright information between the second and third books of poems. "E. Smith of Baileyton, Tennessee," copyrighted Rosemary and Pansies on December 11, 1909, while "E.W. Smith" copyrighted *Rhymes from the Cumberlands* on September 20 of that year. Why the difference in the names?[18] And how had Effie Waller Smith come to claim residency in Baileyton, Tennessee?

In his 1988 essay, "Effie Waller Smith: An Echo Within the Hills," David Deskins developed a racial thesis to support his contention that the E. Smith and E.W. Smith (the "two Effies") are one:

The years prior to her marriage to Charley [sic] Smith were difficult ones for Miss Effie from many perspectives. She lost a brother who was very dear to her. She suffered

17 Elizabeth Engelhardt, "Effie Waller Smith: African-American Poetry from the Breaks," *Appalachican Heritage,* Vol. 36, No. 3, (Summer 2008), 80-83.

18 Deskins, "An Echo Within the Hills," 43.

through a disastrous marriage that ended in a divorce initiated by Effie Waller. She suffered also due to her situation and station and in light of these racial inequities may have reached certain conclusions about life and her art ... the conclusion that there was to be no fair reading for her as a member of the black race. She had to find a way to inject herself into the marketplace under competitive conditions...

With this in mind the literary career of Effie Waller Smith must of necessity be dealt with in two entirely separate periods and ***almost as if we are dealing with two different authors.*** *The first is Effie Waller of Pikeville, Kentucky and the author of* Songs of the Months *and* Rhymes from the Cumberland. *The author of these is a black person, and in each book the author's color is disclosed, discussed, and apparent. The second literary career is as Effie Smith of Baileyton, Tennessee. She is the author of a volume of poems called* Rosemary and Pansies *and other poems and short stories printed in some of the most important and prestigious magazines of the day. The author of* Rosemary and Pansies *is an author of unknown color. From reading the works it can be assumed, though it is never stated, that she is white.*[19] [emphasis added]

In the first blush of my passion for Effie, her life and poetry, Deskins's analysis felt perfect. It explained everything! I imagined a narrative in which her poetry could have flourished during the brief stability and happiness of her courtship and marriage—before all the losses. But the more deeply I went in search of Effie, the more questions I wished I could ask Effie herself.

What bothered me the most was the distinct jump in the level of craft between the poems in *Rhymes* and those in *Rosemary*. Deskins noted in his Introduction to *The Collected Works*: "The poetic forms employed in Rosemary and Pansies are similar to many that Waller used in the past except that they are far more polished."[20]

Who or what explained the deepening of Effie's skills between 1904 and 1909? And why publish two books so close together, within the span of just three months? Nothing I could find satisfactorily explained such a rapid maturing of poetic craft. If the two books had been published even years apart, rather than months, if Effie had not suffered so many devastating events after 1908, I could have believed that she

Who or what explained the deepening of Effie's skills between 1904 and 1909?

had authored both collections. As it was, the abrupt change in the level of craft made me read all of Effie's poems again and again, looking for what proved she had written them all.

Deskins's 1988 essay contains a long and thoughtful introduction to Effie Waller Smith's life and work and some astute analyses of several poems. His case for Effie Waller Smith as the author of all three of the books of poems relies heavily on his narrative of her life (her broken marriage with Charlie Smith, the death of the infant she bore in 1908, and the loss of Marvin, her beloved brother) to account for the contrast between the quality of the poems in the first two books and the third one. The second book, *Rhymes from the Cumberland*, he says,

19 Ibid., 37-38.
20 Deskins, Introduction, 20.

closed a period of her life where Miss Effie as an author had been looking outward toward nature for inspiration, solace, and contentment. And her answers.... The incidents of her life over the next years would force her to look within for answers, and it is then that she matures and ***makes the jump from a rhymer to a true poet*** *in dealing with her ultimate questions.*[21] [emphasis added]

As I read the analysis of Effie's poetry in Elizabeth Engelhardt's *The Tangled Roots of Feminism, Environmentalism in Appalachian Women's Writing,* it struck me that Englehardt focused nearly exclusively on poems from Effie's first two books. Engelhardt declares that the two dominant qualities defining Effie Waller Smith's work are Effie's eastern Kentucky home and her identity as a black woman. However, in "Effie Smith's" volume of poems, *Rosemary and Pansies* and in the short stories, the setting that grounded Effie Waller's early writing is absent. In fact, all three short stories are firmly set in east Tennessee. Further, the poems in *Rosemary and Pansies* contain no references to "the Cumberlands" which Effie Waller loved and praised in her first two books. And in the stories and the third book of poems the author's race is not clear. In fact, as we have seen, Deskins says that "[f]rom reading the works it can be assumed, though it is never stated, that [Effie Smith] is white."

Deskins attributes the authorship of *Rosemary and Pansies* to Effie Waller Smith by a process of elimination: he cannot prove that the book is not by Effie Waller Smith and thus concludes that it must be. The more I read through all the poems, however, the more I struggled with the "two Effies." All of the essential points supporting Effie's publication credits and the narration of her life events arise from what Deskins wrote and published in his essays and his Introduction to *The Collected Works.* No one had carried this work deeper, and no critic besides Elizabeth Engelhardt has done a major analysis of Effie's poetry.

I admire Deskins's work in bringing Effie to light and agree with most of his analysis of her poems, as far as he takes that analysis, but as I studied the poems, his explanation began to feel more and more inadequate. Further, as I read her short stories, I became convinced that the specifics of characters and the east Tennessee location did not feel consistent with what I knew of Effie Waller Smith. Deskins pointed out in the 1988 essay that "[he] wanted to prove, beyond any doubt that the two Effies were only one." He adds, "I never did find conclusive documentation."[22]

I could not rest from my search for Effie's story so long as my genealogical research did not support the narrative David Deskins presents for Effie's life. The gaps bothered me too much. The fact that Effie Smith dedicated *Rosemary and Pansies* "To the Memory of My Brother Marvin" nagged at me. Marvin does not appear in any record of the Waller family. In his Introduction to *The Collected Works*, Deskins addressed Marvin's absence from records of the Waller family in a footnote, reiterating his hypothesis from an earlier essay where he says, "There was mention of her brother Marvin, who was a child hidden and protected by the family, most likely as the result of some deformity or disfigurement."[23] However, he cites no source for this statement.

Effie Smith's poem "My Brother" is subtitled with his dates: "1882-1903."[24] Though it was not uncommon at the time for families to keep a "defective" child isolated even from other

21 Deskins, "An Echo Within the Hills," 37.
22 Ibid., 43.
23 Ibid., 42.
24 Effie Smith, *Rosemary and Pansies* (in *The Collected Works of Effie Waller Smith*), 94.

family members, twenty-one years is a long time to keep a deformed child "hidden and protected." *Where was Marvin?* became my most urgent question.

■ ■ ■

We sigh for human love, from which
A whim or chance may sever
And leave unsought the love of God,
Though God's love lasts forever.

We seek earth's peace in things that pass
Like foam upon the river,
While steadfast as the stars on high
God's peace abide forever.
—*"Forever,"* Rosemary and Pansies

Not always the goal we climb for
Is it possible to attain,
Not always the thing we wish for
Are we able to obtain.

The heights that famous men have reached
We all may hope to reach;
But often the striving for them
Will a noble lesson teach.
—*"Once on a Time,"* Songs of the Months

A narrative of Effie Waller Smith's life that supports her authorship of *Rosemary and Pansies* rests on the existence of a brother, Marvin, to whom the book is dedicated. Though David Deskins says that Effie's brother, Marvin, "appears often in her poems," I did not find references to a brother in either of her first two books.[25] It is only in the third book, *Rosemary and Pansies,* copyrighted by E. Smith of Baileyton, Tennessee, in 1909, that Marvin appears.

But where was the historical Marvin? Finding Marvin became my obsession as I continued to track down Effie's story in calls to Wisconsin libraries and in bibliographies and online catalogues accessed from my office in Kentucky. I belong to genealogical websites that provide search engines for Census data, military records, city directories, and even newspaper articles. I had already used these resources to find Census records relating to Effie Waller. Now I pushed into research for Marvin Waller, at the same time that I widened my search for evidence of Effie Waller Smith in Tennessee records.

I never located any records for Marvin *Waller*. I had known that I was unlikely to find official records, if he had been born, kept and buried at home. I hadn't expected to find a birth certificate, but I thought I might find evidence of a grave or perhaps a death certificate. It did not seem logical that a family as devout as the Wallers would not have a public grave for their beloved son. I also did searches for an infant child born to Effie and Charlie Smith, hoping that perhaps there would be some record—if not a birth certificate, then some record of the burial. Again, I found no record I could link with certainty back to Effie Waller Smith.

What I did discover was a multitude of Effie Smiths! A few in counties near Pike County, Kentucky—one in Lawrence County and another in Martin County—and several in east Tennessee. How could a person ever sort them all out? Even with the miracle of online researching, the searching and sorting might take months—I had already been at this for months!—and never yield an answer. Discouraged, I turned

25 Deskins, Introduction, 6.

again to Effie's poems and stories, looking for some kind of proof that Effie Waller Smith could have written them all, though my conviction that she had faded the more I read. The writing itself pointed toward east Tennessee. There had to be either an Effie Smith in east Tennessee or some record of Effie Waller Smith there.

Late one morning at the end of July, I was ready to quit after a several hours of online research and rereading the poems and stories. I sat down at the computer and rechecked email, then logged onto the genealogy site to give it another try, irritated at myself for not being able to let it go. As I followed possible links for Effie Smiths in Tennessee, I came upon a drawing of a woman in Victorian dress, seated at a desk and bent over her writing. With a shock I read the caption, "Effie Smith Ely was an author of Christian essays and poetry." Another Effie Smith who was a writer! Only this Effie's last name was Ely. But she had come up in a search for Effie Smiths.

The woman who had posted the drawing owned a public family tree, which meant I could open it and see the lines of relationship. If it had not been for this fact, I could not have so easily followed links to discover that this Effie Smith (later Ely) had been born in McPheeters Bend, in Hawkins County, Tennessee, one of a set of twin daughters born to Benjamin and Earnestine Smith, in September 1879, just months after Effie Waller had been born in Kentucky. My heart beat hard as I looked at the 1900 Census record linked to this Effie Smith and read down the list of people in the household: Benjamin F. Smith, Earnestine M. Smith, Effie Smith, Adria Smith (her twin sister), Marvin Smith, Summers Smith. Marvin Smith. Not Waller, but Smith— born in February 1882, the same year as the brother Marvin to whom Effie Smith (the E. Smith of Baileyton, Tennessee) had dedicated her book of poems.

I had found Marvin. And along with him, proof of "the other Effie."

A mix of feelings—dominated by grief—radiated through me. *It's over,* I thought. Everything I had been working toward in my pursuit of Effie—what did it mean now? I stood and backed away from the desk. I didn't want it to be true. Much as I had doubted that Effie Waller Smith had written the short stories, I wanted to be able to prove that she had written the poems. Maybe this Effie Smith in Tennessee, despite her brother Marvin, was not the author of *Rosemary and Pansies.* And yet, the drawing associated with this Effie Smith was of a woman writer.

I returned to the page online where I had found the drawing and searched the family tree owner's other postings about Effie Smith Ely. Within a few minutes I had found "Forever—by Effie Smith Ely," reprinted from *Aspects,* a monthly devotional journal.[26] The same poem appears in *Rosemary and Pansies* attributed to Effie Waller Smith. In subsequent research, I have found the words from "Forever" written by Effie Smith Ely cited on hymnary.org as the words to a hymn included in Methodist hymnals. The accompanying biographical note reads: "Wife of a Methodist minister, Rev.

A mix of feelings—dominated by grief—radiated through me. It's over, I thought.

Joseph B. Ely, with whom she shared the work of rural parishes in the vicinity of Morristown, Tennessee. Born in Hawkins County, Tennessee; educated at Sullins College, Bristol, Tennessee; and in Peabody Normal College, Nashville."[27]

26 Effie Smith Ely, "Forever," *Aspects,* ed. David S. Lampel, Issue 84, (November 1997). http://www.iclnet.org/pub/resources/text/aspects/asp-084.txt.

27 Effie Smith Ely, www.hymnary.org.

This Effie, like Effie Waller Smith, was a Methodist, and, as David Deskins had surmised when he first read *Rosemary and Pansies*, white. Effie Smith married Reverend Frederick Ely in 1920—thus the disappearance of work by Effie Smith in magazines like Harpers and Putnams after 1917. This Effie Smith went on to publish two more books I have been able to locate: *My Mountains* (Nashville: Parthenon Press, 1959) and *Devout Poems* (Bristol, TN: King Print Co., 1969). I also discovered that Effie Smith Ely won the "prize of $20 for the best short story" from the Junaluska Women's Club (in western North Carolina) in 1922, so it seems likely that she also authored the short stories now collected with Effie Waller Smith's writing.

"What are the odds?" Deskins had asked—two Effie Smiths writing at the same time, about the same kind of topics, with very much the same sensibility.[28] It turns out that even at a million to one, there is that one.

I began my search for Effie Waller Smith out of indignation at her silence and her disappearance. As I uncover more about "the other Effie" I realize that her work, too, deserves to be credited to her. What have I done but discover another woman writer lost to all but a few readers? A woman whose life story waits to be told and whose fine work deserves to be understood in the context of that story. A woman writer for Tennessee to claim and celebrate.

■ ■ ■

I think now of those days when hills
And vales with music rang,
Of which in crude, uneven,
Yet rhythmic, words, I sang.

And I am thinking, poet friend,
How you have oftentimes,

Admired with pure unselfishness
Those simple, homely rhymes.
For 'tis the genius of the soul
(Though underneath a skin
Of dusky hue its fire may burn)
Your unfeigned praises win.
Oh that earth had more of beings
With generous minds like yours,
Who alike, true worth and honor
To the black and white secures.

—*from "Answer to Verses Addressed to Me By Peter Clay,"* Songs of the Months

It isn't over, of course. In fact, I am relieved to be able to see "my Effie" more clearly and for the world to be able to assess her important place in the literature of Kentucky, of Appalachia, and of black women writers. Her life and work stand on their own merits and can be seen clearly for the first time. A long detour in our understanding of Effie and her life is ended, and we can begin to tell and retell her story in its truth and fullness.

Elizabeth Engelhardt realized that Effie Waller Smith "wished readers to acknowledge her and her characters as inseparably Appalachian, black, and gendered."[29] Her chapter on Effie Waller Smith as a prototypical Appalachian eco-feminist in *The Tangled Roots of Feminism, Environmentalism, and Appalachian Literature,* as I have pointed out, relies almost exclusively on poems from Smith's first two books—the books we now know that Effie Waller Smith wrote.

28 Deskins, "An Echo Within the Hills," 44.

29 Elizabeth Engelhardt, *The Tangled Roots of Feminism, Environmentalism, and Appalachian Literature,* (Athens: Ohio University Press), 121.

Engelhardt was drawn to poems clearly set in the Big Sandy Valley and on the Cumberland Plateau, in a particular mountain landscape and culture that looks and feels different from other Appalachian cultures. She points out that Effie's poems are for those who love the hills as she does. "Readers who do not understand how important Appalachia can be to a person from Appalachia are not Smith's concern," Engelhardt declares in her commentary on "On Receiving a Souvenir Postcard," one of my favorite poems in *Rhymes from the Cumberland* because of the way the poem describes the Big Sandy River and the young couple sitting on its banks and dreaming of their future.[30] This is a landscape I recognize, with the river at its heart. Though the days of "steamboats/Painted in colors gay" is long gone, anyone familiar with the history of the Big Sandy knows how important they once were to the commerce of the region. The entire scene is authentic for those "insiders" to whom Smith writes.

Engelhardt also notes the power of Smith's poem, "The Hills," another poem that rang particularly true to me. Anyone not from "the hills" cannot really know the feeling they engender in native Appalachians. I was a "brought-on" bride—a woman of the flatlands of western Kentucky—who did not share my husband's (and later my children's) instinctive exhalation of "There they are!" at the spot along the Mountain Parkway where we first sighted the hills in the distance on our way home. Effie captures something of it:

He is not destitute of lore,—
Far, far from it is he,—
Who doth the mighty hills adore,
And love them reverently.
. . .
How sweet among their vales to roam,
And view their summits high;

Here may I ever have a home,
Here may I live and die!
—*from "The Hills,"* Songs of the Months

Many of Effie Waller Smith's poems depict her walking among the hills, free and strong and unafraid. Effie made the trip to the Breaks of the Mountains near Elkhorn City, Kentucky, many times, glorying in the steep gorges and high crags of stone. It is difficult territory to navigate and treacherous, still, to climb, but Effie loved it. Though she was a black woman, she "[enacted] a vision of how safe the world should be in the face of how dangerous it often was."[31] It was this spirit I sensed in her portrait that January evening. A spirit not found in the more somber and death-obsessed poems of the Effie Smith who wrote *Rosemary and Pansies.*

Further, in "The Hills," Effie Waller Smith links her Appalachian home to the larger world of literature in which she also roamed and read with ease. She manages to include echoes of Wordsworth and allusions to Shakespeare as she conjures a landscape worthy of its own art and music:

The wondrous works of God I view
In every dell and nook;
And daily learn some lesson new,
From Nature's open book.

Here calm and wooded glens afford
The noblest, purest kind
Of inspiration for the bard's
Dreamy and gifted mind.

30 Ibid., 122.
31 Ibid., 125.

And here is music never still,
Not tiresome, weird or dull;
And here are scenes for artist's eye,
Lovely and beautiful.

■ ■ ■

The Effie Waller who wrote *Songs of the Months* probably could not have imagined the Effie Smith who would grow old in Waukesha, Wisconsin, and finally die in her adopted daughter's home in Neenah. And yet, her need to live the free and safe life her poems envision led her and her mother to move north. Effie Waller Smith followed her faith and sought to live it out with the Metropolitan Church Association. The extremes of that sect eventually began to tear it apart and caused many of its adherents who, like Effie, had given the church everything they owned to sue for some of it back.

What we want doesn't always take us where we imagine it will, as Effie found out more than once—as all of us realize sooner or later. I imagine, though, that Effie would look back on her life (as I am looking back on my life lately) and decide that on the whole what we wanted had been trustworthy. That when we committed ourselves to something—a faith, a family, an art (whether it be writing, teaching, gardening, or friendship)—it brought us deep satisfaction. Through uncertainties and blind alleys, life finally comes down to "falling down nine times and getting up ten." As simple as taking the next step, which is to step into your own life more deeply. Effie was one who knew

What we want doesn't always take us where we imagine it will, as Effie found out more than once—as all of us realize sooner or later.

how to keep on walking. Looking for Effie brought me back to the habit of daily writing, following her I wrote my way into a new place.

Effie made her life count. She used the best part of her years to enact the changes she wanted to see—through her teaching, her writing, and living her faith. She may have despaired that culture and society could never change except by means of the deepest and most individual changes of heart—the kinds of change she wrote about and sought in her own life. Death, betrayal, injustice, sin—these would always be in us and so, with us, unless we turned our thoughts to God. Ignorance, however, did not have to persist. Teaching might change things. Friendship might, and loyalty mattered, too. "Doing what you can"—that, she trusted—and most of all, her God. At least these are my thoughts as I read her poems.

I am grateful for Effie Waller Smith's poems that capture the calm wild beauty of the eastern Kentucky mountains and something of the life she lived as a black woman of spirit, intelligence and determination in Appalachia at the turn of the twentieth century. Effie's writing allows us a glimpse of a more racially complex Appalachia than we may have imagined. As her poems continue to be read and studied in the context of their time and place, her place in the literature of the region will be more fully appreciated. Her courage and persistence, her grace and loyalty live on in her poems.

David Deskins writes of the "enormous rock garden" Effie created in Waukesha during the 1930s. This garden with "hundreds of different varieties of blooming plants, flowers, and shrubs" became, he says, her "form of public expression." A poetry in plants and stones which she tended until 1950 when her health began to fail. Thousands of visitors signed the ledger she kept. This garden allowed her to surround herself with something of the beauty she had found all those years ago in the Breaks of the Mountains on the Kentucky-Virginia border—and to share it with others as she had shared the Breaks in her poems.

More important for the future of our understanding of Effie Waller Smith and her work, it appears that she did continue to write. Deskins mentions in passing that "a stationery box containing poems reveals that she maintained a very private interest in poetry throughout her life."[32] It is impossible to calculate what those poems might reveal of Effie's growth as a writer. Though I have not seen the poems, nor have I been able to locate them, I am certain that we will have them someday. I look forward to the time when writers and scholars can read and discuss Effie's late work, but for now I am content to know that they exist.

Again and again Effie Waller Smith's poems declare what mattered to her—and what did not:

The tranquil peace and happiness
That sweet contentment brings,
... is not

... for those who daily walk
The crowded ways of life
Eager for gain and eminence
Though won and held through strife.[33]

There is an unbroken quality to Effie's life that lifts her from the ranks of poets perhaps more famous or even more skilled than she and proves that she has more than earned her place as a distinguished poet of Kentucky. ■

32 Deskins, Introduction, 9.

33 Effie Waller Smith, "A Mountain Picture," *Rhymes from the Cumberland* in *The Collected Works of Effie Waller Smith*, 23.

NIGHT IN THE BURNED HOUSE

In my old bedroom, in this house
now my Aunt A's, walls mottle grey

into black, char hiding that this room
was ever painted purple in a hope

that someone *would guess*, would know.
Burning night, my hidden journals

blown across the field—and my aunt,
gathering boughs for wreaths, found

I love him. I have not seen her eyes
since. She who sang hymns with me

as we hung the wash, who said
you can tell the Lord anything, and me too—

David and Jonathan a holy story,
but my love *a wickedness.* All night,

I press hands to these walls, whisper
what I cannot say without a flower

opening, a disappearing boy, a house
burning. Let the morning never come.

LUCIEN DARJEUN MEADOWS

HOLLER

Growing up, we lived down in a holler, and sometimes,
Coyote loped through our fields—nothing to eat but okra
And tomatoes—before crossing dirt road to Baker's farm.
Sometimes, a scream unlimbing chicken. Sometimes,
gunshot

And silence. When we moved in, neighbor Johnson spoke
Low to Father: *You got a gun? Here, you are your own*
police.
Only trees will hear you holler. But when storms crashed
through,
Father and I would cross treeline to stand fieldbare,
breathing

Bloodscent of wet earth, my red toes reaching like roots
into dirt,
His black hair plastered over shoulders and back like
wolfmane,
To howl and holler into lightning, our voices thick with
thunder

As we watch mountains close around us, push back olive
sky,
Sacrifice some hilltop sycamore so only rain comes
running
Down here: flashriver, summerflood, wash our holler out.

LUCIEN DARJEUN MEADOWS

BOOK REVIEW

Kathleen Driskell. *Next Door to the Dead: Poems.* Lexington, Ky.: The University Press of Kentucky, 2015. 102 pages. Softcover. $19.95.

Reviewed by Marianne Worthington

Kathleen Driskell's new collection of poems is not only an affable invitation to walk among the dead in a graveyard but also an arresting testament on the art of poetry, the writing process, and the caging of creativity manifested in poems that are surprising and wholly satisfying. Part of The University Press of Kentucky's "Kentucky Voices" series, *Next Door to the Dead* advances beyond the Horatian platitude that poetry should both instruct and delight into a meditation on harvesting the imagination. In the second of two poems titled "Ars Poetica" the specters in this poem could as easily be provender for poems as they might be ghosts in the graveyard: "I have summoned them / but hold them / in the low sky / above the churchyard. // Moored, they tug against my greed, / my imagination. / I know I could let / them go, / but / no, not / yet, no." With grace, ingenuity, and attention to poetic craft, Driskell has set her poems to bloom and thrive outside of the confines of any cemetery.

But that is where we begin: inside the literal graveyard next door to where Driskell and her family have made their home in a pre-Civil War Lutheran church house for over twenty years. One of the distinguishing marks of the poems in the first half of the book is the use of funerary imagery. Angels, tombstones, caskets, and epitaphs punctuate the themes of the poems, of course, but also spur admiration for the poet's gifts for shaping language. Mourners in black are "the heavy / notes of a dirge." Buzzards gathered around a dead deer at the edge of the cemetery become "the greasy black prayer-circle," "the dark congregation," the "pallbearers / who will lift high the deer into the grave / weeping sky." In these poems that introduce us to the poet's local landscape the dead "rise up / and float as if angel-food." Meanwhile, we are kept aware of the poet's intentions to chronicle these graveyard stories. While hanging laundry on the line in "Markers," the speaker watches a man dig a grave while pinning "up the corners of my blank white sheets," a "blank to be filled in."

As the poems move us outside the iron gates of the graveyard we continue to contemplate our own confinements, our own humanity. In "Inishmore, Aran Islands" the speaker says (using a lovely echo of the long e sound):

> *I see in myself what could not be seen*
> *until considering these squared green fields:*
> *the rolling land has been caught seized,*
> *fenced by its own stony elements.*

Another excellent example of this rumination on enclosures (temporal, corporeal, and poetic) is the long poem "Tchaenhotep" that helps to center the collection. Tchaenhotep is a mummified middle-class Egyptian housewife brought to Kentucky after the 1904 St. Louis World's Fair and now housed in the Kentucky Science Center. In an interview with her publisher, Driskell said, "I began my relationship with her [Tchaenhotep] years ago after accompanying my children on grade school field trips to the Louisville Science Center.... I thought about her for years before I believed myself ready to write a poem about her." Tchaenhotep's poem is a first-person account of her life and death and afterlife that reflects on the themes of subjugation. On being confined as a housewife in the ancient world, she says, "my husband's heart was lean / and stringy. He eyed me as if I were something to eat / and he was a wild dog on the streets." On being (literally) wrapped up: "... for centuries I lay in the dark. // ... For two thousand years, I waited for the door to open, / and when it did, the sun lit / but another pyramid on the stone wall." On being a dead thing on display: " ... but no one asked me to speak, / I was only told

With grace, ingenuity, and attention to poetic craft, Driskell has set her poems to bloom and thrive outside the confines of any cemetery.

to be / still, here, there, / faces and faces leaning in / close, their sour living breath blowing over me. / Why be a god if you are but a thing / to be so coarsely regarded?"

Driskell's excellent poetic commentary on themes of enclosure is amplified through the rest of this collection. The latter half of the book includes (mostly) either persona poems spoken by the dead or poems spoken by the living as they contemplate their dead. All the while, we are made aware of the poems as a type of container for stunning imagery, subtle rhyme, and diction appropriate to the speakers. In "Death of the Civil War Infantryman, Mill Springs, Kentucky," for instance, the soldier speaks as he is dying in the mud. His speech is clipped, disjointed—a sort of death rattle—as he watches red birds light on the tree limbs above him: "The sky. Gray. Infinite. / Approaching. Each bird, sudden, unexpected, like / sudden blood blooming through the chest." Another compelling persona poem is "From the Grave of the Mathematician," a cleverly imagined and skillfully crafted sonnet. The mathematician contemplates the crosses on tombstones as plus signs as well as the "equal signs / that wagon wheels leave in the mud / when carrying an infant's coffin." In "Epitaph: For the Man with No Last Name" the poem is spoken by a group of "God-fearing" gravediggers who find and bury a stranger with his belongings expect for a "dear John" letter which they nail "to that hickory / tree over yonder" and from which they learn the dead man's only name: Ned. The poem is short-lined and shaped like a grave. In another grave-shaped poem the actual grave speaks to the poet (and to the reader), beckoning us to "stop / here, lean / in, put / your ear / near. // Nearer, nearer / still and / I'll tell / all. Of course, we practically do fall into this grave/poem as we're brought closer and closer to our own mortality.

Next Door to the Dead ends as it begins, with the arrival of birds patrolling the skies above the graveyard. In "Flock," masses of birds are "swirling and swirling above / they are / stirring the soup of love," until they perch in the trees, "each branch / like a road leading to the heart / of a town I had not known / I wished to visit." At the very least, Kathleen Driskell's poems inspire us to get out and visit our dead but more than that, the poems offer praise to "this dark / nourishment,

/ imagination." In language both opulent and adroit she gives voice to the forgotten and calls us to witness our own inevitable demise. ■

William Wright. *Tree Heresies*. Macon, Ga.: Mercer University Press, 2015. 65 pages. Softcover. $18.00.

Reviewed by Rosemary Royston

Tree Heresies is a collection of poetry whose music often conjures Hopkins and at times Dickinson, yet the music is fully Wright's. Images allow for a hint of narrative: the troubled psyche of a sleepless narrator, a silent father, a toothless woman, a burning attic, and the tension of the pastoral alongside the anti-pastoral. This tone of the book is best captured in the title poem's description of the narrator's dream, "...trust this / music to destroy the freight of definitions...," as the music and imagery of these poems ask the reader to inhabit the speaker's ability live in two landscapes—the waking life and its torments, and the landscape of the dark dream-world. The reader sleeps alongside the speaker in "Sleeping Underground," as he "dream[s] of cities...," "grandfather's hawklike eyes," and "fallow fields, scorched leaves" while turning in his grave-like bed.

Opening with "Prologue," which is like a primer to the collection, the reader walks with the narrator, "tak[ing"] a road into a place you do not know—," where "owls crouch the limbs spirit-eyed to watch / for mouse-skitter or skink..." While there are signs of beauty, "home to plum and scuppernong," the overlying tone is that of a portentious landscape as the scene becomes foreboding, "...A swamp stagnates, impaled with a derelict / truck, mattresses, a charred tractor and heaps of cattle bones." The walk continues through "An earth left igneous, ignored," through "Ghost-choked country. / Where no ear / stops for story, lest metaphor siphons bible tongue, / lest image shake loose weathers to kill the seed." The final destination is at a "brown Victorian house" with a large porch and "immaculate sadness," where "Upstairs, she turns in her pain." This "she" is followed by the "he" or the narrator himself, in the final section of "Prologue," looking back "...houseward to the high window," the woman inside "a nun to her lost son."

As the collection unfolds, the poems rotate through the landscapes of nature and the psychological, such as the authentic description of cicadas in "Nocturne for Cicada," whose music "at times...lodges in the ear like a burr," to the brutally grim, as in "Nightmare, Revised," where an "eviscerated" father has been "sewn back to life," and a family turmoil is revealed. Woven in and out of the poems are allusions to the Bible, whether the genesis moment, "bible tongue," or the sparrow in "Lantern Sparrow," where a common sparrow lands on "a lone flue" of a homestead that's burned down. The speaker has "entered a sadness I had never felt before," yet the simple sparrow, the "ghost-sparrow, sparrow of country roads gone / to the snowlight of spilled milk," allows the speaker to envision a time when he "would ask it nothing about the night / only savor its clarity, its warmth in my hands."

A recurring motif in this collection is that of an attic—a burning attic, a collapsing attic, an attic that the sparrow might "haunt." From "Attic and Image," "Furnace and Fox," to "Summer Insomnia," the reader encounters the attic and its metaphorical weight, always collapsing, burning, or sagging—the threat of a psychological weight that can destroy; a weight that already keeps the speaker up at night. In "The Book of Nights," the weariness of the speaker's inability to sleep is captured in "half-heard whispers that seize the dark / threads of sleep from my eyes with surgical / care." Comparing sleep to drowning, the speaker fails to succumb, as "...summer's green gears / grind the heart to such friction that it scalds, / it sears the center: The clock's hands burn..."

The second and final section of *Tree Heresies* is "Infloresence," and the poem of the same name addresses yet another walk the speaker takes, "...past all / praise and grief, motion, murder." Yet again, spring arrives in April and "triggers its trillion ways to house a flower," with the sun, "that cataclysmic star." While the poems still chronicle the dark, there's a resolution of sorts, a coming to terms as in "Eight Essays on a North Carolina Farm, 1920," where the farmer and his wife are given a brief close-up on the farm, in the kitchen, "Both of them old / before their time, // work-torn..." The ghosts in these poems never truly depart, and the speaker comes to know the heart of a "black wolf" in the penultimate poem, "Question." His connection with this wild wolf is profound, and as he watches her return to the "barren wood," he feels "an absence // so complete that, just then, / I would have followed her into death." It is this liminal space that many of these poems inhabit, calling the reader to return to the grave-like bed, the burning attic, the call of the cicadas in order to be there with the speaker on this dark and potent journey. ■

RECLAMATION, KISS

In the slash-back of Kentucky, our prayers always for rain,
  rain
curling into cyclone, rain in leaky

milk jug, in boot, in whiskey barrel.
Rain survived and rode on

passed steel silt tracks, run over and over
like road-kill too mangled and severed to resurrect itself,

rain scissored
into field, cropped, mulched, prayed over,

sang to and measured.

MARYELIZABETH POPE

CRAWDAD

Aged and wrinkled as barn noosed tobacco, as toe tips of
leather, icing
coolers of algae crusted pints and rocks

slipping and swishing warm slime through melting arctic
until dinner was salty brown sea-sediment

like backwashed creeks floating drowned bait traps
regardless of days melted

hammering each seam open.
We'd feast week-long on bedrock, anoint the urchin

with lemon, suck and smack juice from weathered
peppered skulls,
shoot the ocean white lightening and all in one gulp.

Dwindle the evening spinning, spinning
until one of us swims down.

MARYELIZABETH POPE

CONTRIBUTORS

Carey Gough's images are contemplations on the point in which documentary photography mingles with poetry, cultural memory, and mythology. Her work has been exhibited in both the United States and the United Kingdom, and has been featured on vice.com, *Oxford American*'s Eyes on the South, and RawFile. She has a BA First Class Honours in Photography from Hereford College of Arts and an MFA in Documentary Photography from the University of Wales, Newport.

bell hooks (née Gloria Jean Watkins) is among the leading public intellectuals of her generation. Her writings cover a broad range of topics including gender, race, teaching, and contemporary culture across the literary genres and include the seminal *Ain't I a Woman? Black Women and Feminism* and, more recently, *Appalachian Elegy: Poetry and Place.* She has taught at Yale University, Oberlin College, and the City University of New York, and has served as Distinguished Professor in Residence in Appalachian Studies at Berea College since 2004.

Marcia L. Hurlow, professor of creative writing at Asbury University in Wilmore, Kentucky, is the author of five collections of poetry. Her most recent chapbook, *Green Man in Suburbia*, won the Backwards City Review Press contest, and her full-length collection, *Anomie*, won the Edges Prize at WordTech. Her poems have appeared in various journals, including *Poetry, Poetry Northwest, Nimrod, Poetry Wales, The Iconoclast, Hawaii Pacific Review,* and *Malahat Review.*

Leatha Kendrick is the author of three volumes of poetry, including her most recent, *Almanac of the Invisible.* Her poems and essays have been widely anthologized, and she is a two-time recipient of the Al Smith Fellowship in Poetry from the Kentucky Arts Council and has received fellowships from the Kentucky Foundation for Women. Her MFA in Poetry is from Vermont College of Fine Arts, and leads workshops at the Carnegie Center for Literacy & Learning.

After growing up on a blueberry farm in Virginia, **Jessi Lewis** has devoted herself to storytelling. She has an MA from James Madison

University and an MFA in fiction from West Virginia University. Her work has been published in *Flyway* and *Ghost Town,* and is forthcoming in *Rock & Sling.*

Kathleen Brewin Lewis is a Georgia writer whose chapbook, *Fluent in Rivers,* was published in 2014 by FutureCycle Press. A two-time Pushcart Prize nominee, her work has appeared in *Valparaiso Poetry Review, Still: The Journal, Yemassee, Heron Tree, Cider Press Review,* and other publications. She is senior editor of the online journal *Flycatcher.*

Lucien Darjeun Meadows's poetry has appeared in *West Branch, Hayden's Ferry Review,* and *Quarterly West.* An AWP Intro Journals Project winner, he has been nominated for the Pushcart Prize and received recognition from the Academy of American Poets. Meadows lives in Fort Collins, Colorado.

Originally from rural Pennsylvania, **Lydia Munnell** lived in Cleveland before heading west to pursue her MFA in Fiction at Bowling Green State University. She is currently the fiction editor for *Mid-American Review.*

Beth Newberry is a writer and editor living in Louisville, Kentucky. Her work has been published in *Sojourners, Still: The Journal,* and *The Louisville Review.* Her essay "The Center of the Compass" was named a notable essay of 2010 by Robert Atwan in the 2011 *Best American Essays.* She writes at thehillville.com.

Maryelizabeth Pope's poems have been published in *Still: The Journal, The Fourth River, One Trick Pony Review, New Madrid, Skinny Dipping, Ballard Street Poetry Journal, Ozone Park,* and elsewhere. Her honors include a 2014 Pushcart Prize nomination and an Artist Enrichment Grant from the Kentucky Foundation for Women. Originally from Harlan, Kentucky, she lives in Louisville with her husband and two daughters.

Divya Ramesh is a junior in the College of Arts & Sciences at the University of Pennsylvania, studying Psychology, Hispanic Studies and Creative Writing. When she is not treading water studying for her exams, she enjoys writing poetry and short stories.

Rosemary Rhodes Royston, author of *Splitting the Soil* (Finishing Line Press, 2014), resides in northeast Georgia. Her poetry has been published in journals such as *Southern Poetry Review, NANO Fiction, The Comstock Review, Main Street Rag, Coal Hill Review, Flycatcher, Still: The Journal, Town Creek Review,* and *Alehouse.*

Jane Sasser's poems have appeared in *The Sun, North American Review, Journal of the American Medical Association,* and other publications. She is the author of two poetry chapbooks, *Recollecting the Snow* (Main Street Press, 2009) and *Itinerant* (Finishing Line, 2009). She teaches English literature and creative writing at Oak Ridge High School.

Conor Scruton is a Tennessean currently living in Bowling Green, Kentucky. His work has appeared or is forthcoming in *Off the Coast, Red Paint Hill Poetry Journal, Gravel,* and other publications.

Pamela Murray Winters lives with her husband and various animals in a house on the Chesapeake Bay. Her poems have appeared in *The Gettysburg Review, Gargoyle, Beltway Poetry, Fledgling Rag,* and other publications.

Marianne Worthington is co-founder and poetry editor of *Still: The Journal.* She is author of the chapbook *Larger Bodies Than Mine,* winner of the 2007 Appalachian Book of the Year Award. Her work has appeared in *Grist, Shenandoah, Appalachian Heritage, 94 Creations, Pine Mountain Sand & Gravel, Kudzu,* and many other publications. She lives, writes, and teaches in southeastern Kentucky.